CW00543018

LOGO MONDO

Hitoshi Nagasawa + papier collè

LOGO MONDO by Hitoshi Nagasawa + papier collè

First published in Japan in 2006
by Graphic-sha Publishing Co., Ltd.
1-14-17 Kudankita, Chiyoda-ku, Tokyo 102-0073 Japan

English edition published in 2007
by Rockport Publishers, Inc.

First published in the United States of America by
Rockport Publishers, Inc., a member of Quayside Publishing Group
100 Cummings Center, Suite 406-L, Beverly, MA 01915-6101
Telephone: (978) 282-9590 Fax: (978) 283-2742
www.rockpub.com

ISBN-13: 978-1-59253-395-4
ISBN-10: 1-59253-395-7

10 9 8 7 6 5 4 3 2 1

Cover Design	4 Eyes Design [www.4eyesdesign.com]
Text Layout	Hitoshi Nagasawa, Masakuni Araki [papier collè]
Editing	Hitoshi Nagasawa, Masakuni Araki, Makiko Inishi, Eriko Takahashi [papier collè]
Overseas Research	Makiko Inishi [papier collè]
Editing Assistance	Keita Fukasawa
Research Assistance	Joachim Fischer [Brand Affairs]
Project Planning and Development	Kumiko Sakamoto [Graphic-sha Publishing Co., Ltd.]
English Translation Management	Língua fránca, Inc. [contact@lingua-franca.co.jp]

Printed and bound in China

preface

For the most part, typography appears to have a predetermined look. However, the historical waves of each generation have rocked and molded even this seemingly stable world.

In the mid-1980s, when graffiti made its appearance in the New York City subways alongside hip-hop, many "adults" frowned, reluctant to tolerate what they saw as shameful and filthy scribbling.

Today, after the plan to clean up New York had been devised, rendering the subways safer and causing the graffiti to disappear, the graffitists of twenty years earlier now bear the honor of having been pioneers, and graffiti art books are being published worldwide.

The reason conservatively minded people harbor fear or horror of "the unknown" is simply because they tend to regard their own culture, which is familiar to them, as the sole legitimate culture. Being content with this single culture creates a sense of safety. Conversely, the young tend to oppose the times, are attracted to the new and novel, and seek to win out over the generation before them.

However, this is the sole source of originality.

Members of the Dadaist movement, which appeared in the early twentieth century, would cut out printed letters to deconstruct words. The psychedelic movement destroyed the "clean" and pristine beauty of conventional Swiss typography. Movements originating in the streets, whether punk or hip-hop, destroyed existing aesthetics and forms. In that respect, the history of typography as it is traced from the Bauhaus to Swiss typography may perhaps be regarded as legitimate, while typography associated with youth culture movements that followed could perhaps be viewed as deviations.

Thanks to Macintosh, the popularization of the personal computer gave rise to the personalization of information as well as the personalization of design and typography. It is engendering personalization in a host of other manners as well.

Personal typography, the diametric opposite of Swiss typography aesthetics, is not universal. Numerous typography designs coexist. This is the current state of typography.

Just because all fields in the design world are constantly affected by the trends of the day does not mean that design consistently advances in a single direction. Minimalism, which enjoyed popularity in the fashion industry in the late 1990s, also caused a revival of Swiss-style typography, and much attention was paid to "flat design" and "nondesign." The year 2004 marked the beginnings of a clear change in direction. Ornate styles, as represented by neobaroque and bohemian, soon made a tremendous comeback in the fashion industry.

The same trend began to take place in typography, as well. In particular, after techno fonts took the world by storm in the 1990s, nondesign minimalism dominated typography. In other words, focus continued to be on a plain, consistent aesthetics. Then the new wave of graffiti appeared to sweep through typography.

Today, the musical genre of hip-hop, which shares commonalities with electronica, has become popular. Graffiti has also mixed with other elements, such as gothic, or goth. Now in typography we see extensive use of stenciling, and it seems that we are on a quest to create a new world.

This book contains all of these new experimentations. We selected typography, icons, and illustrations that display novelty and, if possible, offer foreshadowing into the next age. We included nostalgic entries, as they hearken back to when these styles played their role as the avant-garde of the day.

Therefore, not all of the book's entries represent today's latest designs. In this field, it is not unusual for a design created in 1996 to appear fresher than one created in 2005. We selected a wide a range of genres because it is impossible to discuss today’s segmented aesthetics using only a few styles.

While we focused on Japanese graphic designers, we did try to touch on graphic designers worldwide as much as possible and included some examples of their work. There are numerous famous designers. However, they are mixed in with more obscure or anonymous designers.

Our criteria for "beauty" comply with our intentions for this book and are not defined by the designer’s level of fame. However, while these criteria seem obvious, they have not been recognized sufficiently throughout design history.

This book begins taking the perspective that graffiti and indy fonts are not merely the results of children playing but that they are outstanding creations. This is not a question of distributed "quantity." First and foremost, it is a question of whether or not a particular design is creative. Consequently, we had no alternative but to exclude some works by famous designers.

We did this because future styles will be created by today’s nameless.

Hitoshi Nagasawa

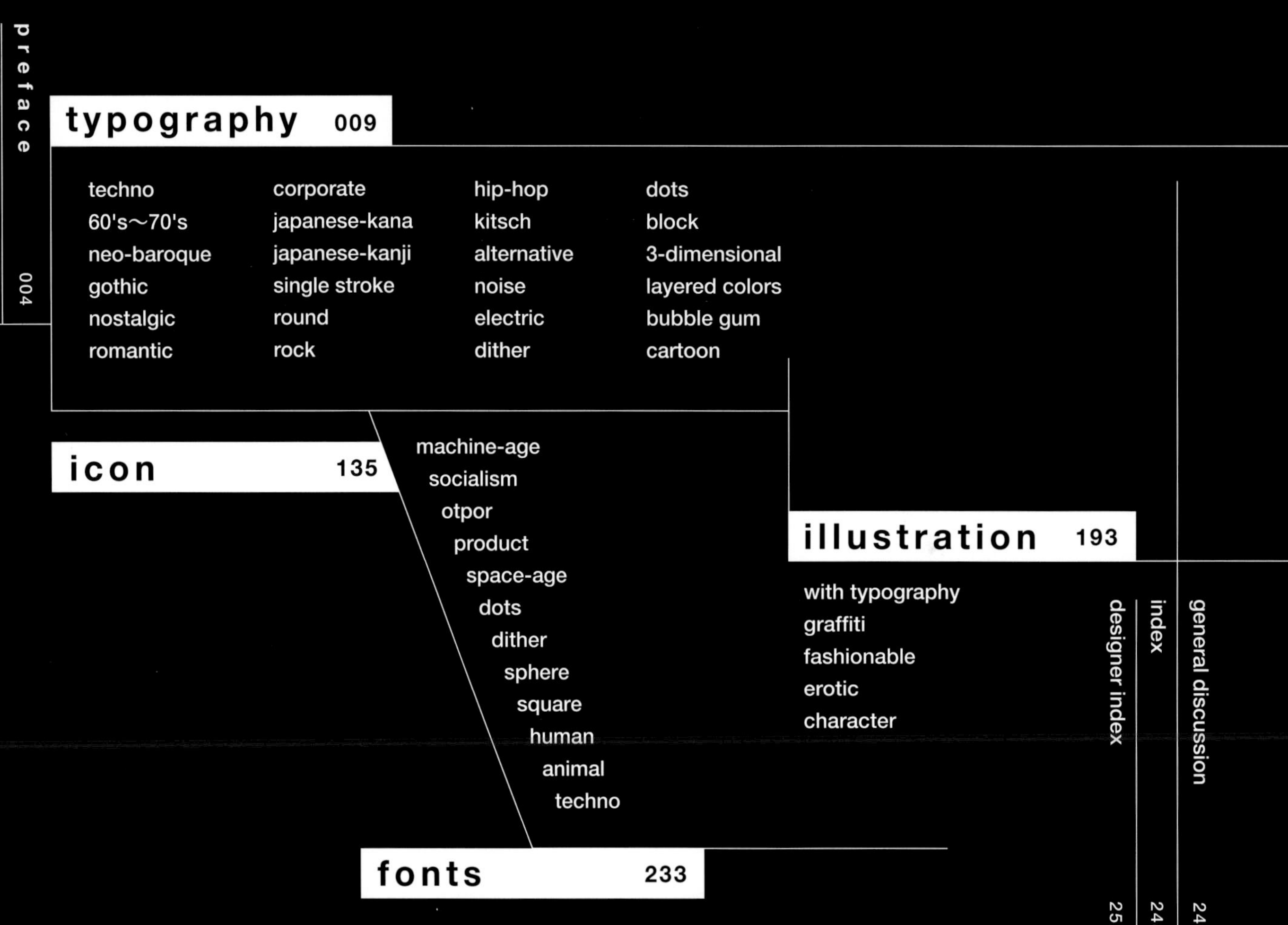

typography

0001

WILDMAN'S HOUSE
ele-king presents
SUPER ROCK
near
future
digi
A.M.
APE vs MO'WAX

0002

0003

0004

0005

g studios inc.

0006

0007

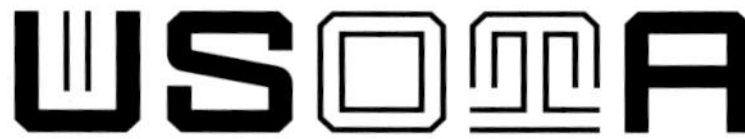

0008

0009

ELECTRONICA
PERSPECTIVE

0010

0011

0012

0013

0014

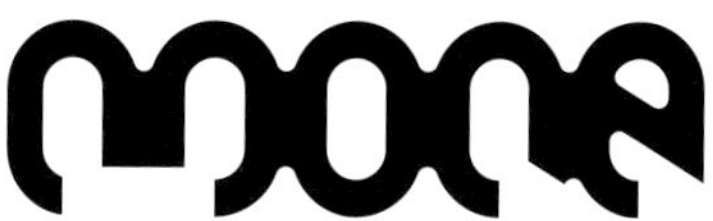

0015

0016

0017

0018

0019

0020

mikro man

0021

REIZ
GERMANY

0022

0023

vagabond

0024

0025

0026

0027

0028

LINKUP!

0029

0030

0031

0032

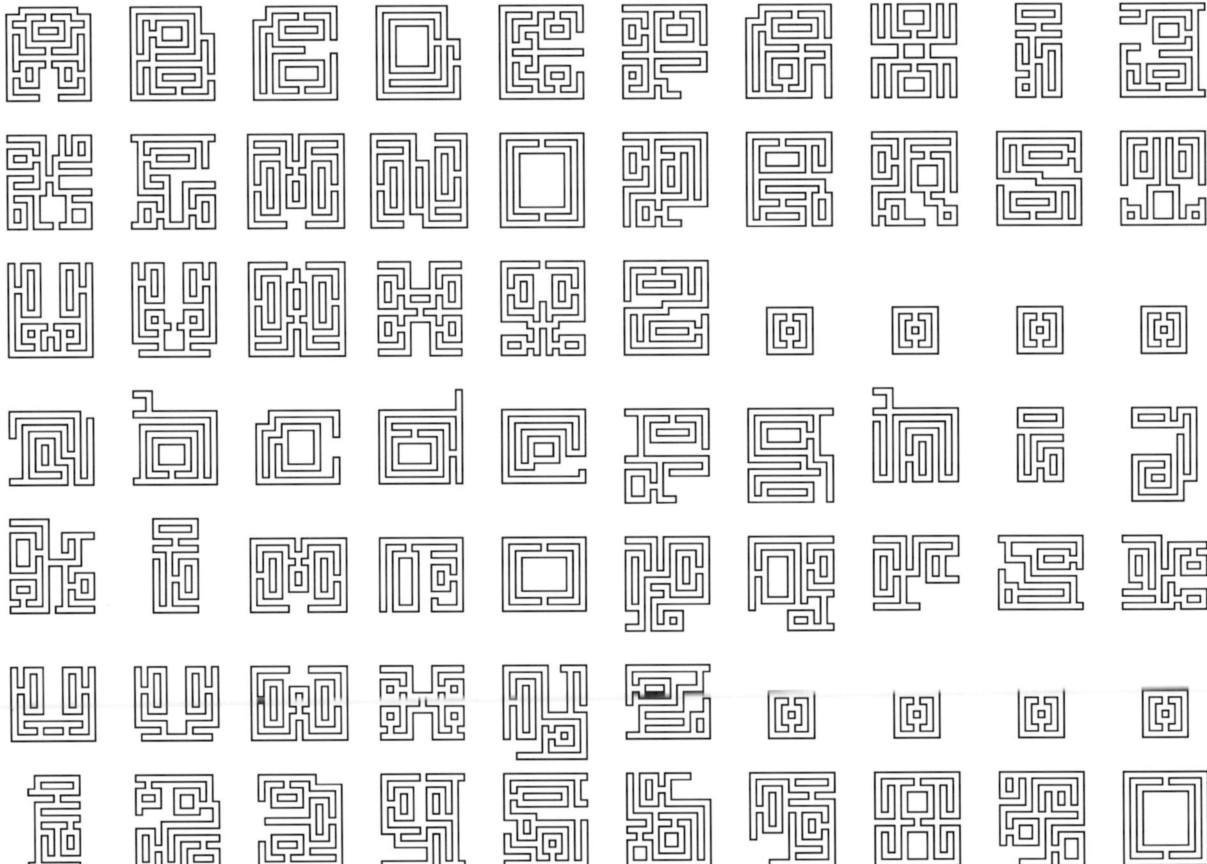

0033

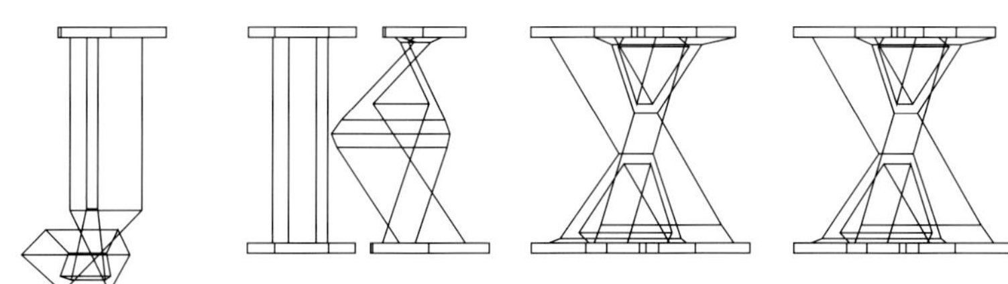

0034

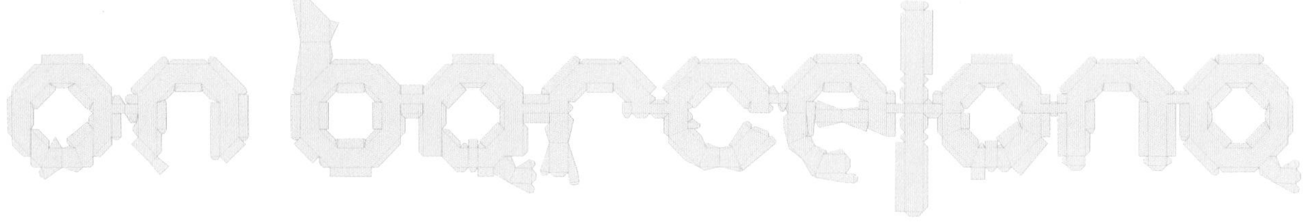

0035

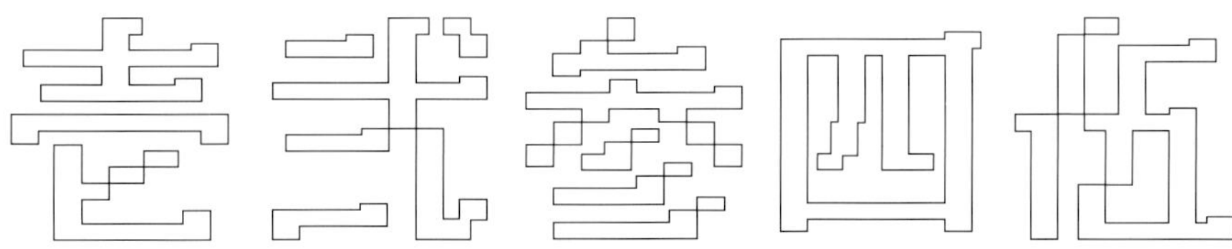

0036

0037

0038

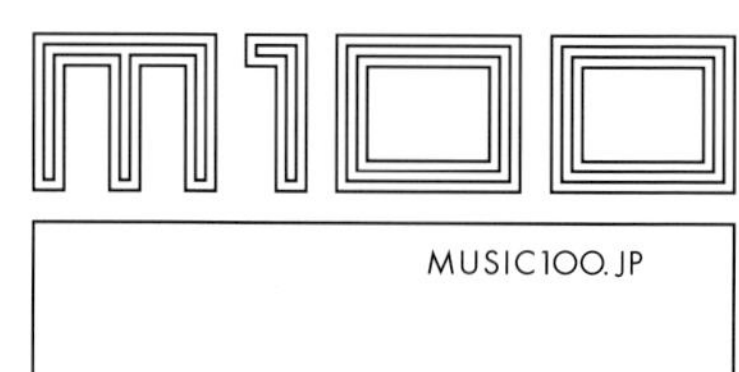

0039

0040

0041

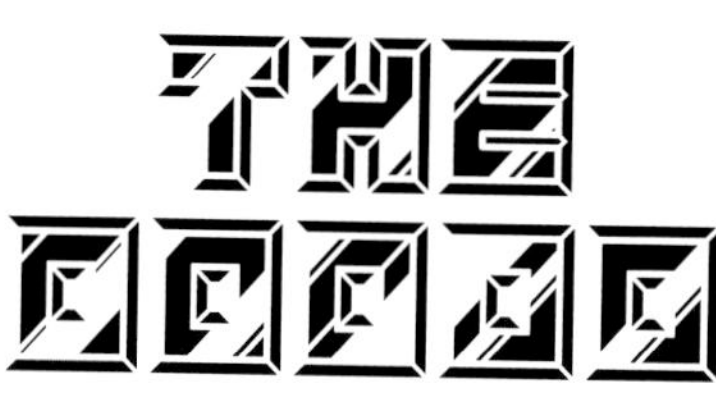

0042

0043

0044

0045

TECHNO
psychedelia

0046

0047

FUNK WARS

0048

0049

ASTRO- .COM

0050

MON TUE WED THU
FRI SAT SUN

MON TUE WED THU
FRI SAT SUN

1 2 3 4 5 6 7 8 9 0

0051

0052

0053

g studios inc.

0054

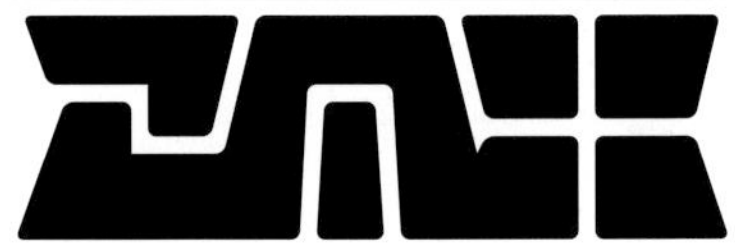

0055

0056

SQART™ » SQART™ » SQART™ » SQART™ » SQART™ » SQART™ » SQART™ » SQART™ »

0057

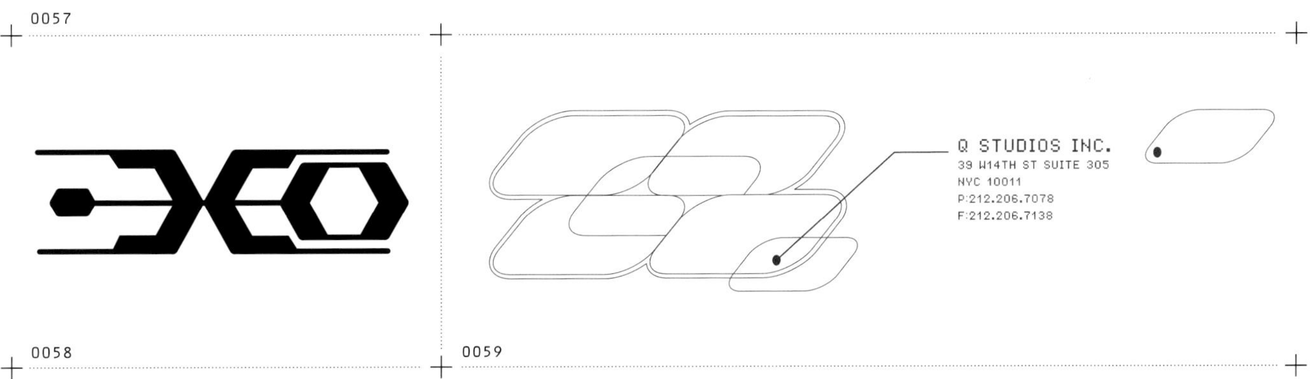

0058

0059

0060

0061

0062

0063

0064

0065

the skate vibe

0066

0067

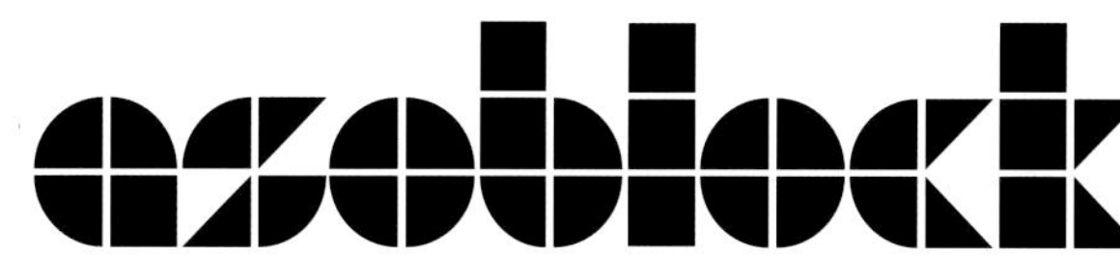

0068

0069

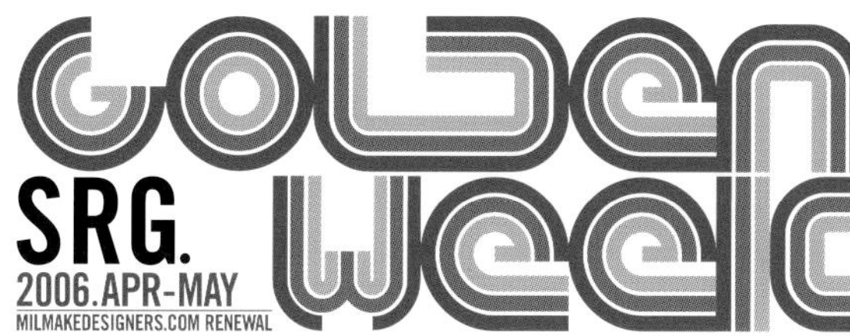

0070

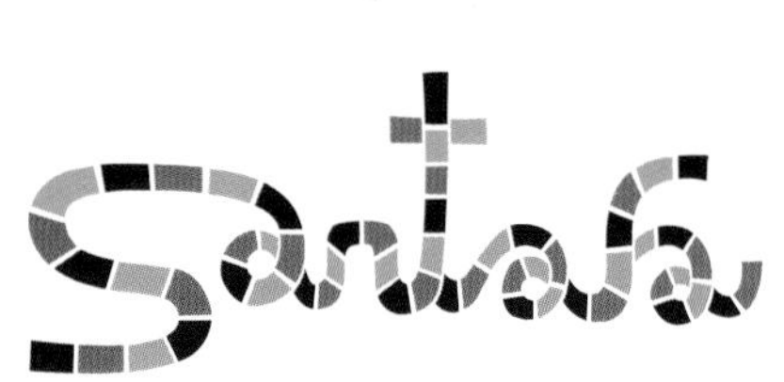

0071

0072

0073

0074

0075

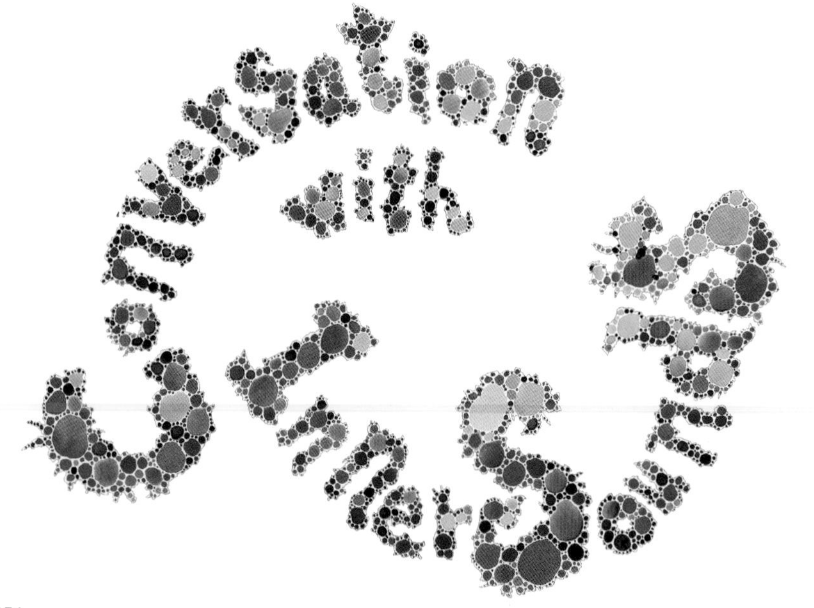

0076

Monochrome

0077

TOKION MAGAZINE PRESENTS CREATIVITY NOW CONFERENCE TOKYO

0078

YURA YURA TEIKOKU

0079

0080

0081

0082

0083

0084

0085

0086

0087

0088

0089

0090

0091

0092

0093

0094

0095

0096

0097

0098

0099

Wannabee Chinese!

0100

0101

0102

0103

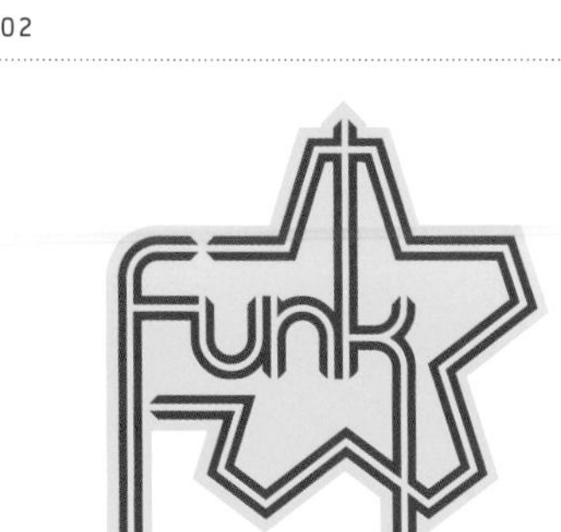

0104

0105

0106

0107

0108

0109

0110

0111

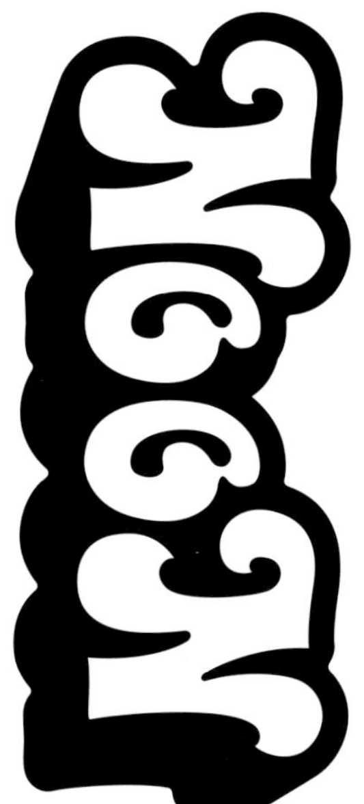

0114

SPEECH
BOYZ

0112

Cutles
MUSIQUE

0113

0115

0116

0117

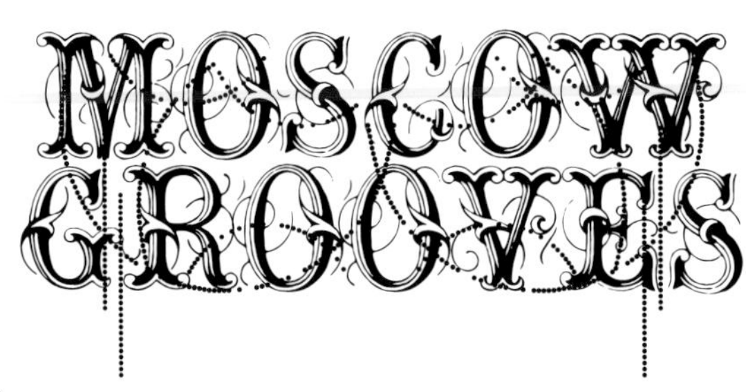

0118

0119

0120

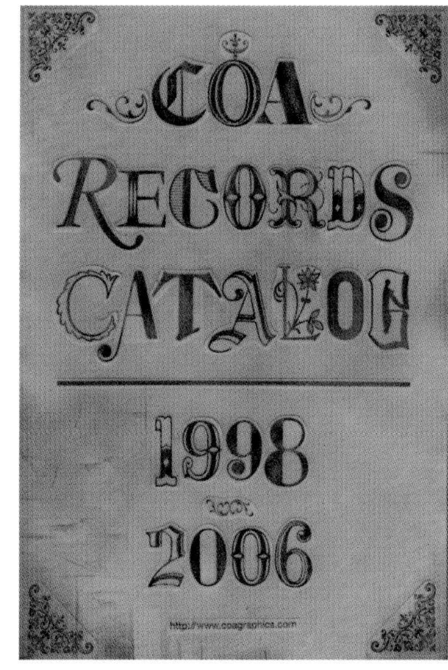

0121

0122

0123

0124

0125

0126

0127

0128

0129

0130

0131

0132

0133

0134

0135

0136

0137

0138

0139

0140

0141

0142

0143

0144

0145

0146

0147

0148

0149

0150

Sigmar Polke

0151

0152

0153

0154

0155

0156

0157

0158

0159

0160

0161

0162

GRAPHIC

0163

0164

0165

0166

0167

0168

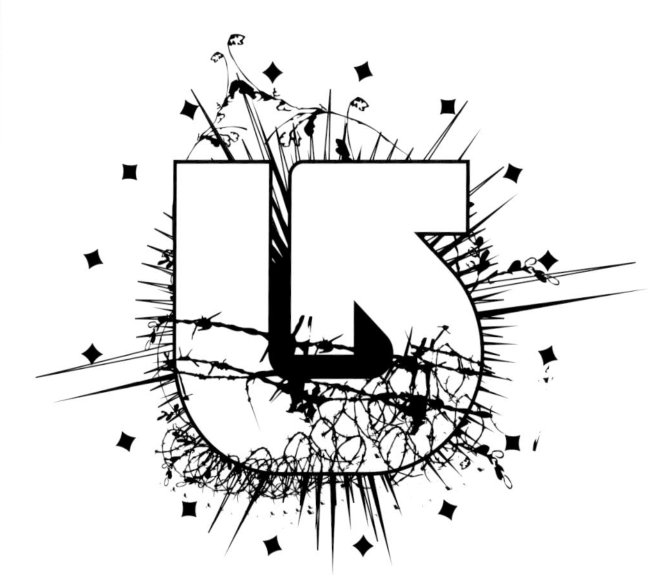

0169

0170

0171

0172

0173

0174

0175

0176

0177

0178

0179

0180

0181

Little emo

0182

0183

0184

0185

0186

0187

0188

0189

0190

TRIP

0191

0192

holden

0193

0194

Purejam

0195

Visual Language

0196

Little emo

0197

Beautiful Streamline

0198

0199

TOKYO BOSSA NIGHT 2005 AT GLASS SQUARE

0200

AUGUST

0201

STATE OF THE ARK

0202

MARSMOBIL

0203

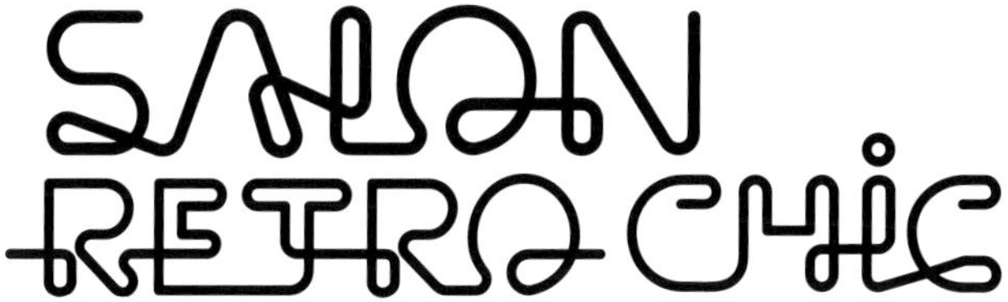

SALON RETRO CHIC

0204

saturday night Ride

0205

organic electronics

0206

FRESH AUGUST

0207

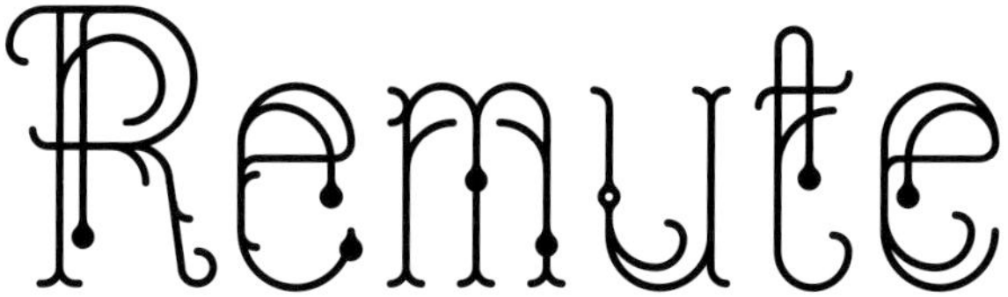

Remute

0208

minimum vibration

0209

0210

0211

0212

0213

0214

0215

0216

0217

0218

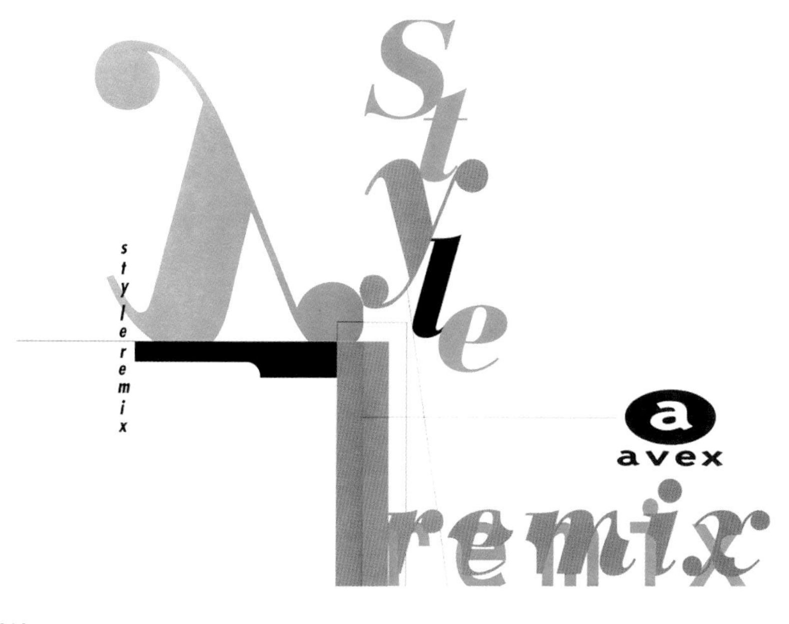

0219

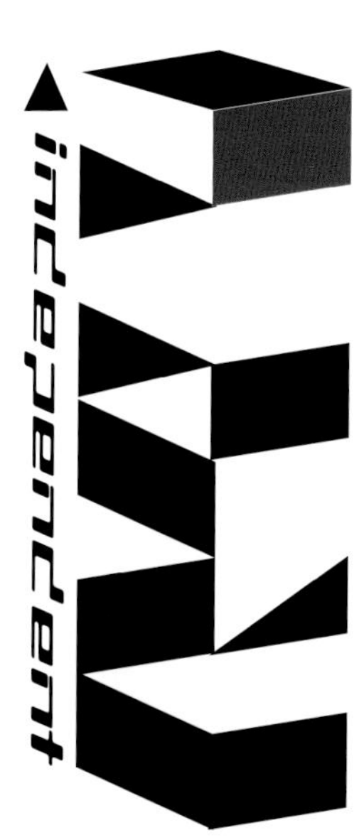

0220

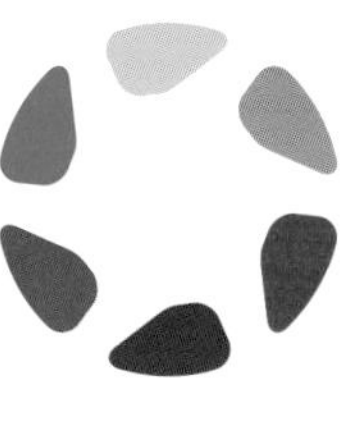

0221

0222

0223

0224

0225

0226

0227

0228

Balloons

0229

0230

0231

0232

AMP

0233

0234

beltane

0235

0236

Coniglio®

0237

0238

STARS

0239

0240

Juell

0241

0242

Incredible

0243

Bowery
Kitchen

0244

0245

0246

0247

frill
R317
is
Here

0248

0249

Kazamidori

0250

0251

0252

0253

0254

0255

0256

0257

0258

0259

DOUBLE FAMOUS

0260

0261

0262

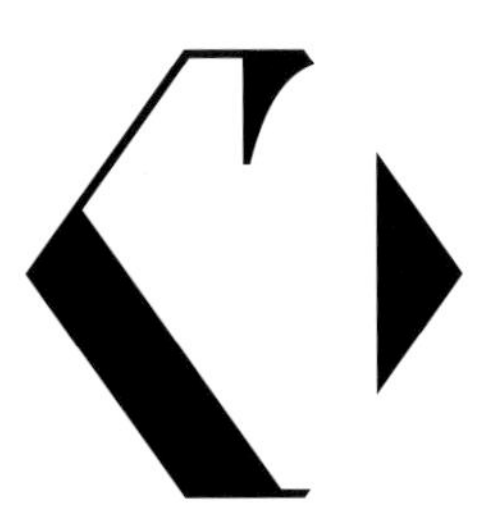

0263

Razzoodock

0264

PREJEXLINE
RECORDS

0265

0266

0267

24HR™

0268

0269

0270

0271

0272

0273

0274

0275

0276

bite

0277

0278

Tar
lum®

0279

0280

mlk W&D

0281

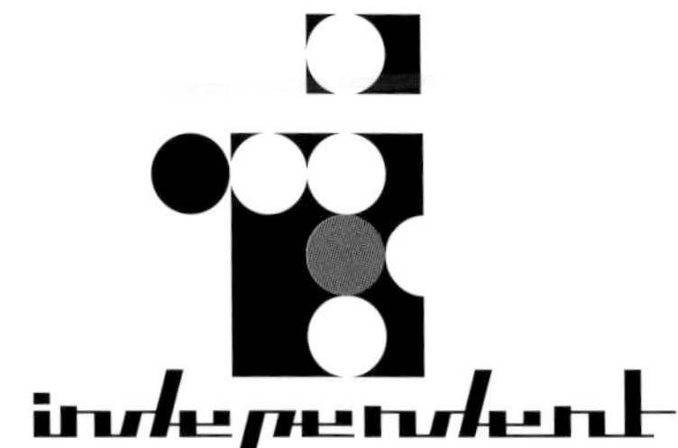

0282

burton

0283

0284

0285

0286

0287

0288

0289

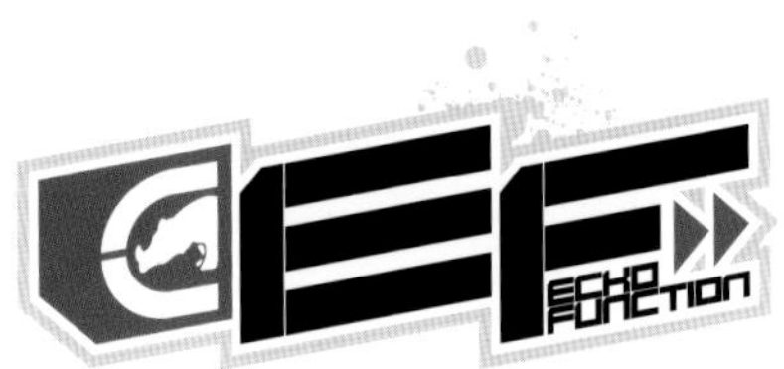

0290

0291

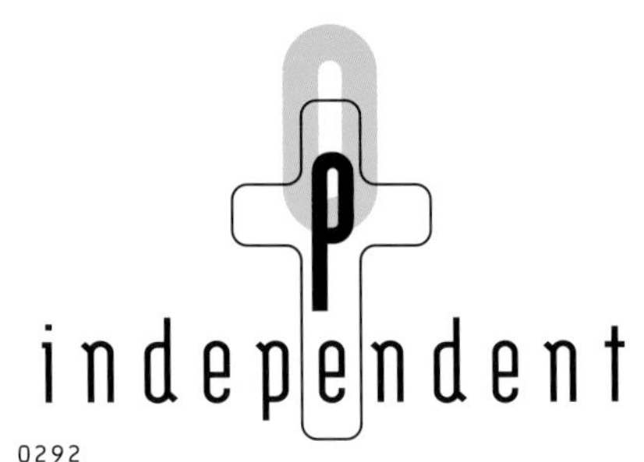

0292

wave ceptor

0293

Jet Maric Go-Around

0294

0295

0296

0297

0298

0299

0300

0301

0302

papier collé

0303

0304

0305

0306

0307

0308

ハイライター

0309

0310

ファンキービジネス

0311

0312

0313

0314

ゲームの楽しさを
教えてあげたい!

0315

交響詩篇
エウレカセブン

0316

電気グルーヴ・ジェネレーション!

0317

0318

コバーン

0319

ファンクウォーズ

0320

いっしょ

0321

0322

マサヨ

0323

0324

はまのくらし

0325

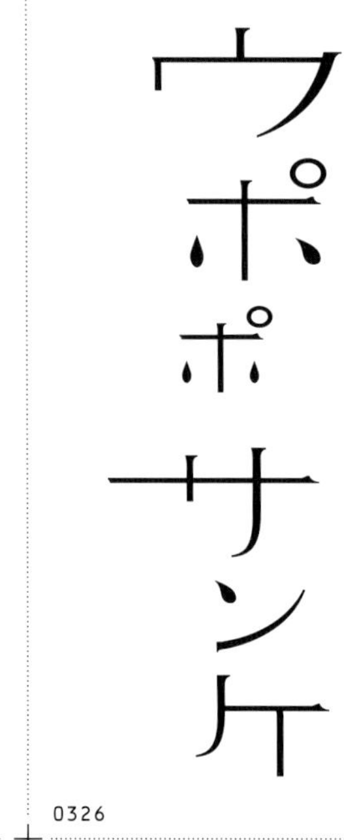

0326

ユキビデオ

0327

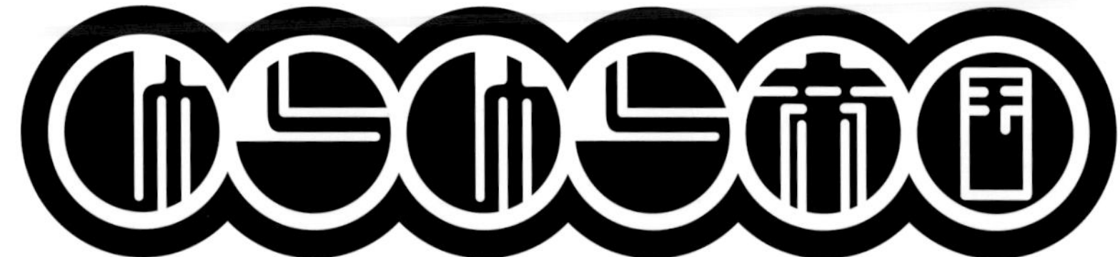

0328

ジャパニーズグラフィックス

0329

0330

モンスター

0331

0332

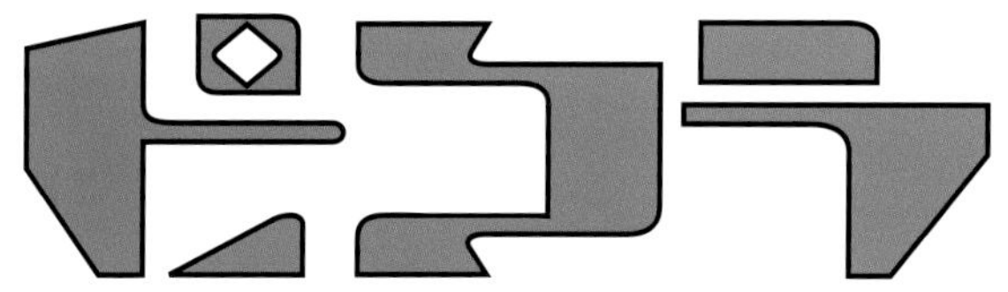

0333

スネイワマンショウ

0334

0335

0336

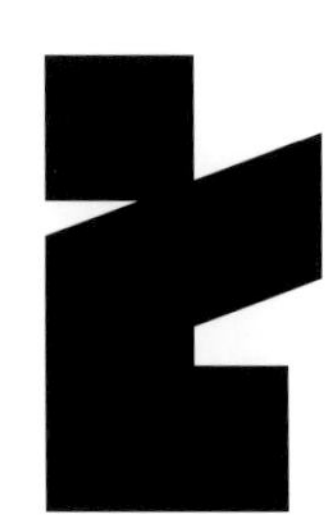

0337

0338

0339

0340

0341

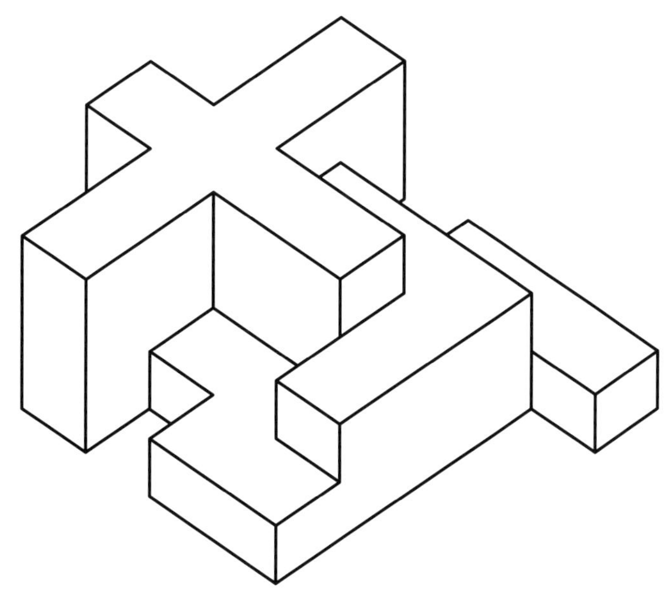

0342

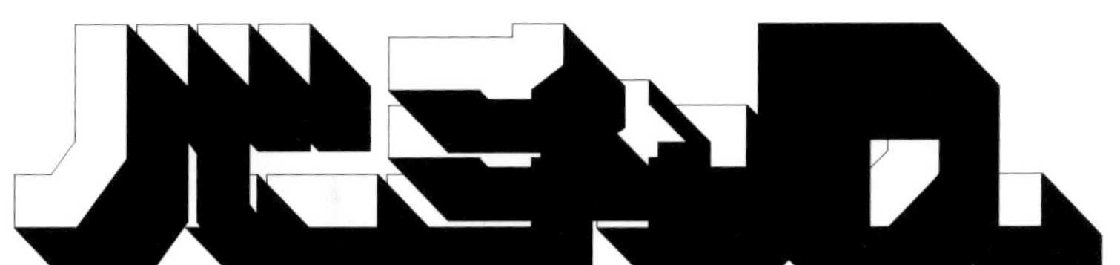

0343

0344

0345

エル・キング

0346

ジャムキャラ

0347

0348

0349

0350

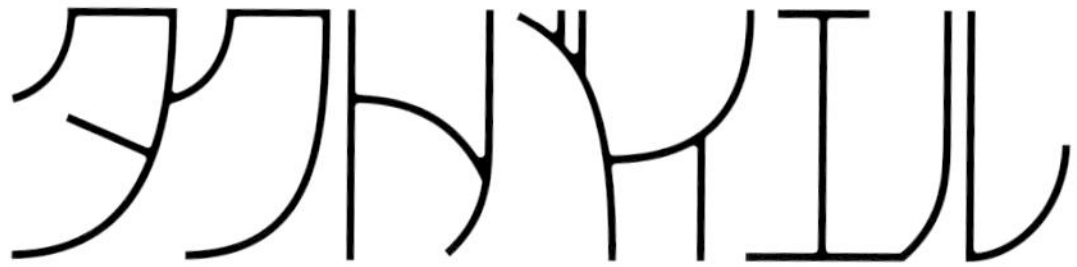

タクトバイエル

0351

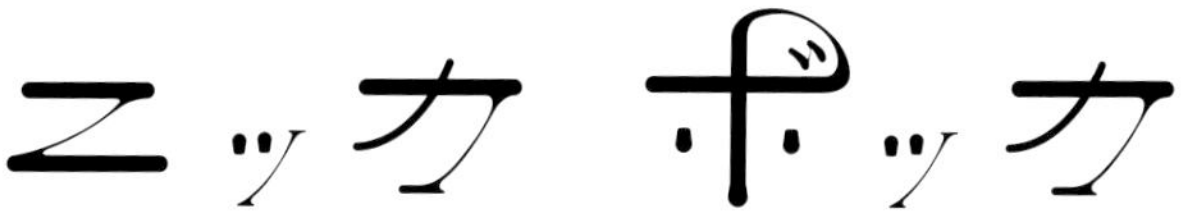

ニッカ ポッカ

0352

ツメマルクン

0353

ペーパーヌード

0354

ナキムシのうた

0355

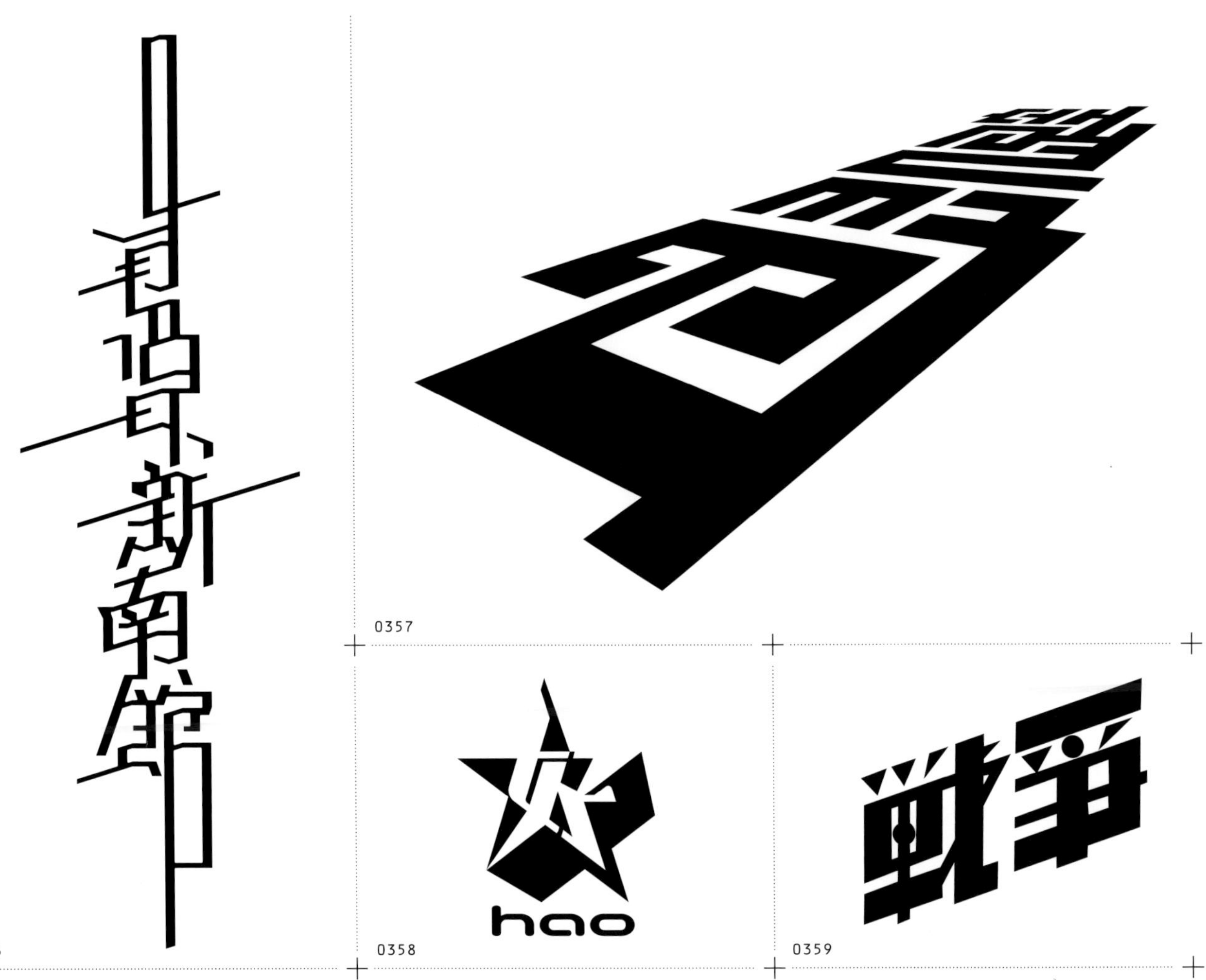

0356

0357

0358

0359

0360

0361

0362

0363

0364

0365

0366

0370

0367

0368

あかねぞら
こいねこの
やまい

0369

0371

ニンゲン、今日モ赤ナ除ク。

0372

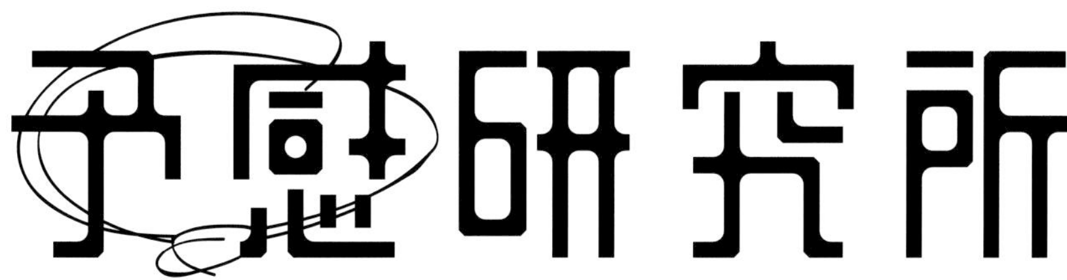

0373

0374

0375

0376

0377

0378

0379

0380

0381

0382

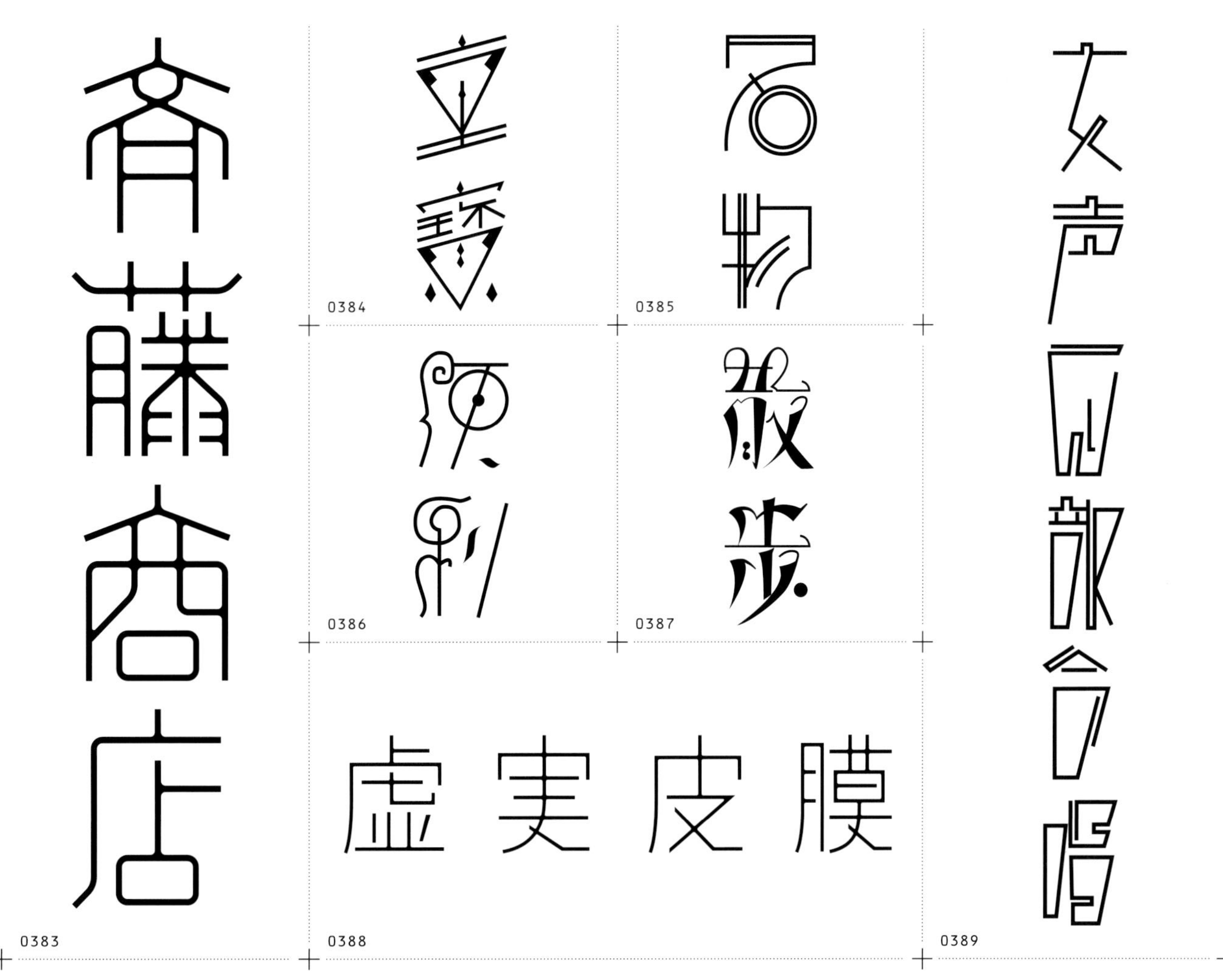

0383

0384

0385

0386

0387

0388

0389

0390

0391

0392

0393

0394

0395

0396

0397

九月十八日、新南館

0398

0399

0400

増上寺景光殿

0401

0402

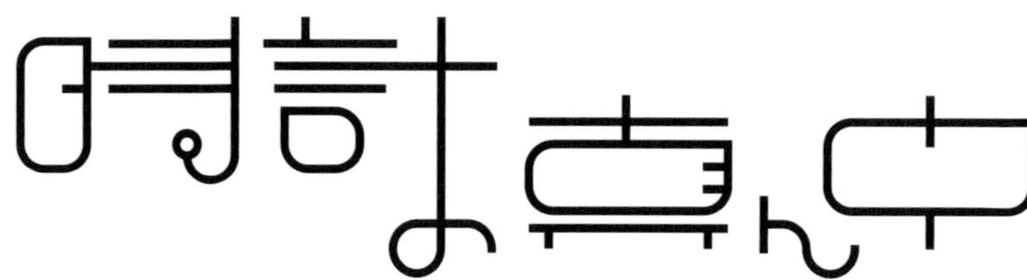

0403

0404

0405

0406

0407

0408

0409

0410

0411

0412

0413

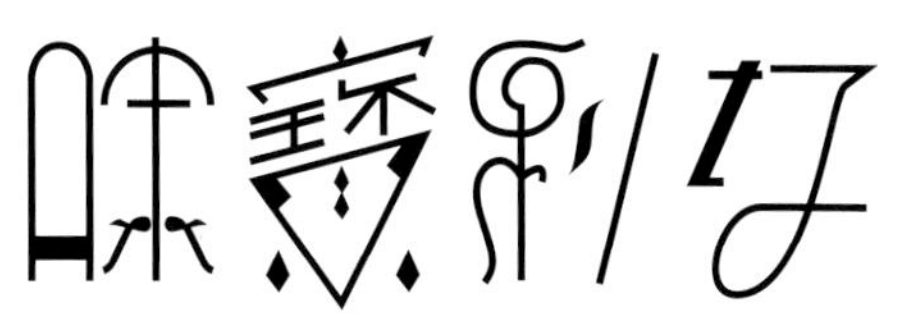

0414

0415

0416

0417

0418

0419

0420

0421

0422

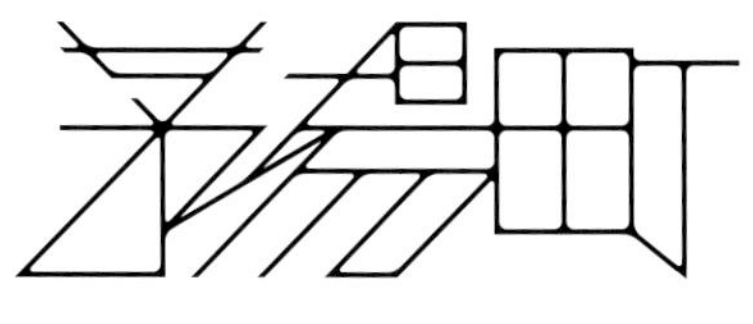

0423

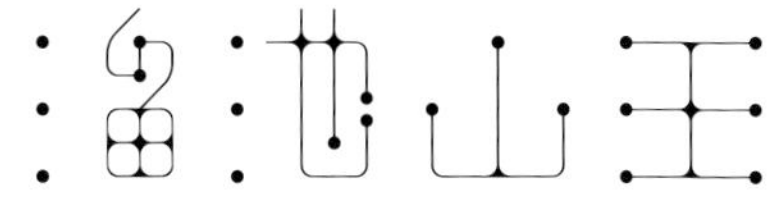

0424

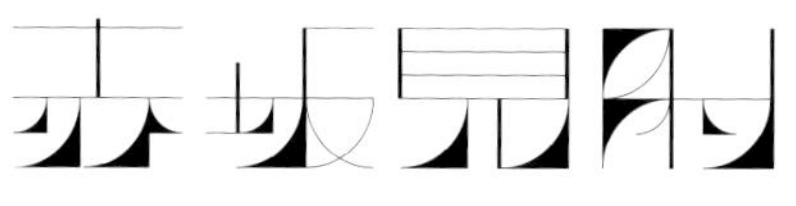

0425

0426

0427

0428

0429

0430

0431

0432

0433

0434

0435

0438

0436

0439

0437

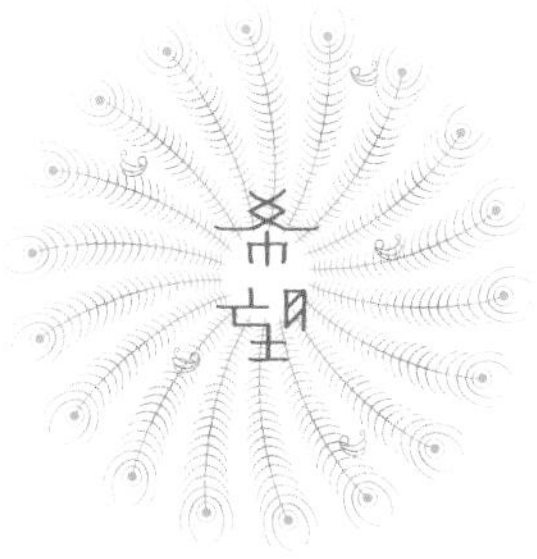

0440

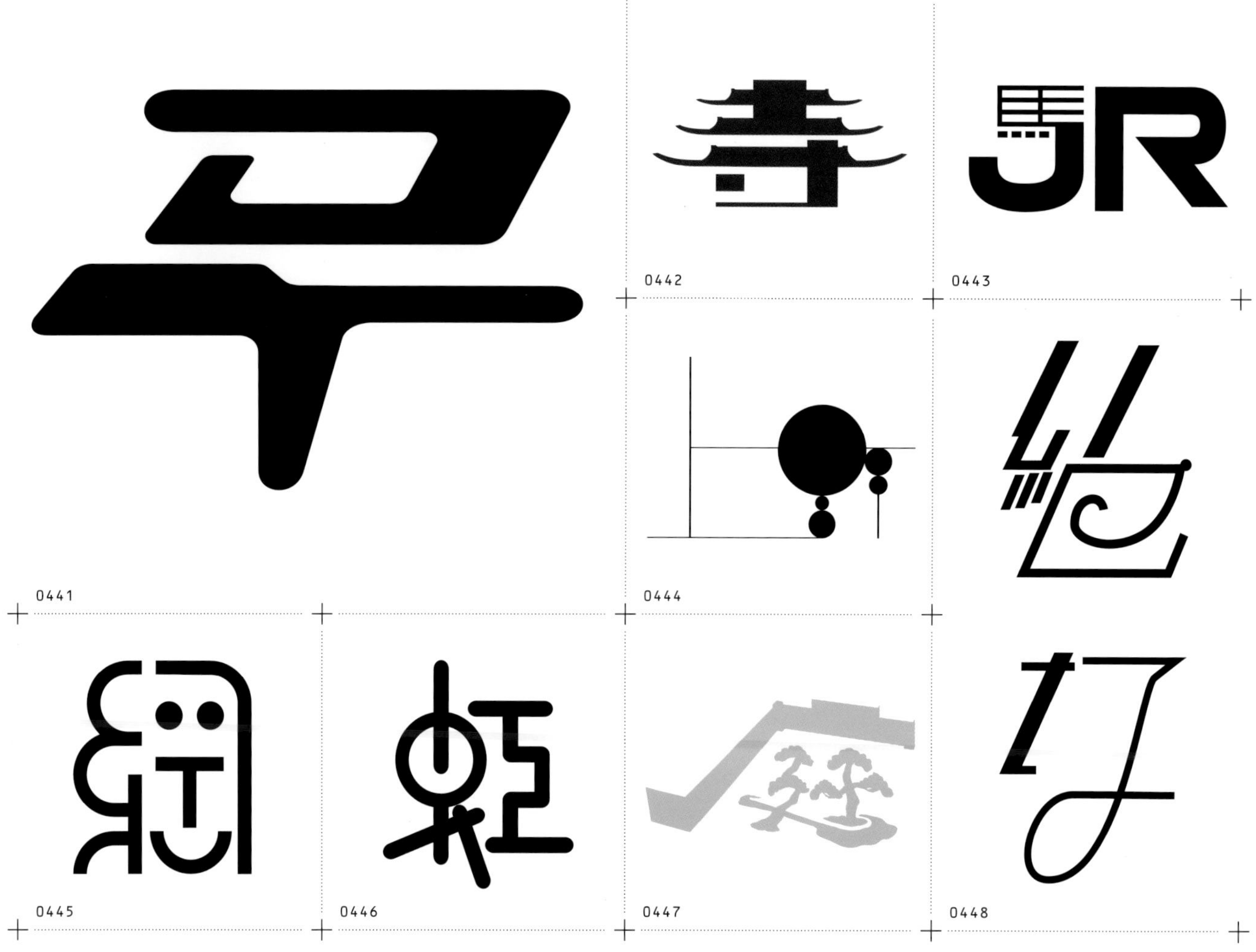

0441

0442

0443

0444

0445

0446

0447

0448

0449

0450

0451

0452

0453

0454

0455

0456

東京
トホトホ
紀行

0457

0458

0459

0460

0461

0462

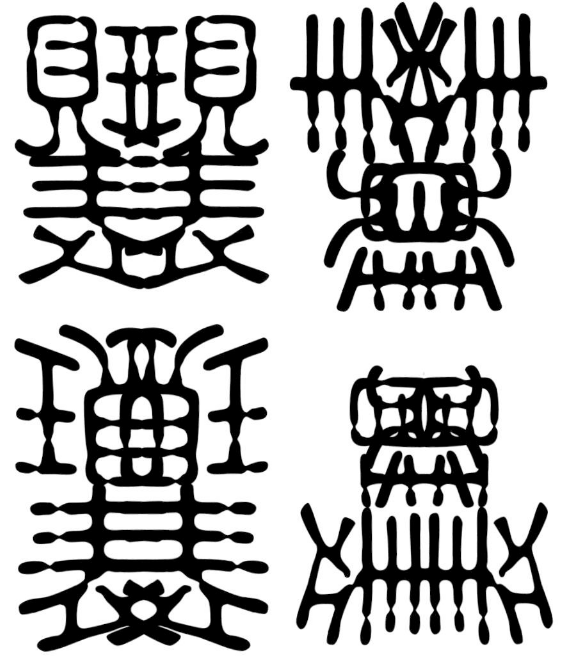

0463

0464

0465

0466

0467

0468

0469

0470

0471

0472

0473

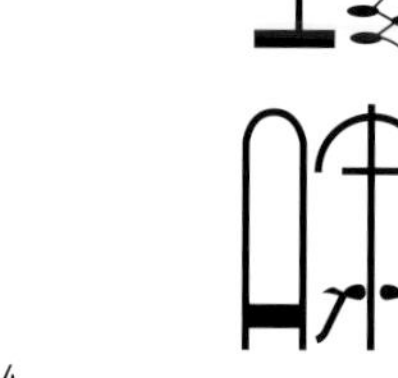

0474

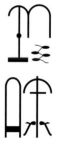

Neighbourhood

0475

0476

Rolling

0477

Common thread

0478

0479

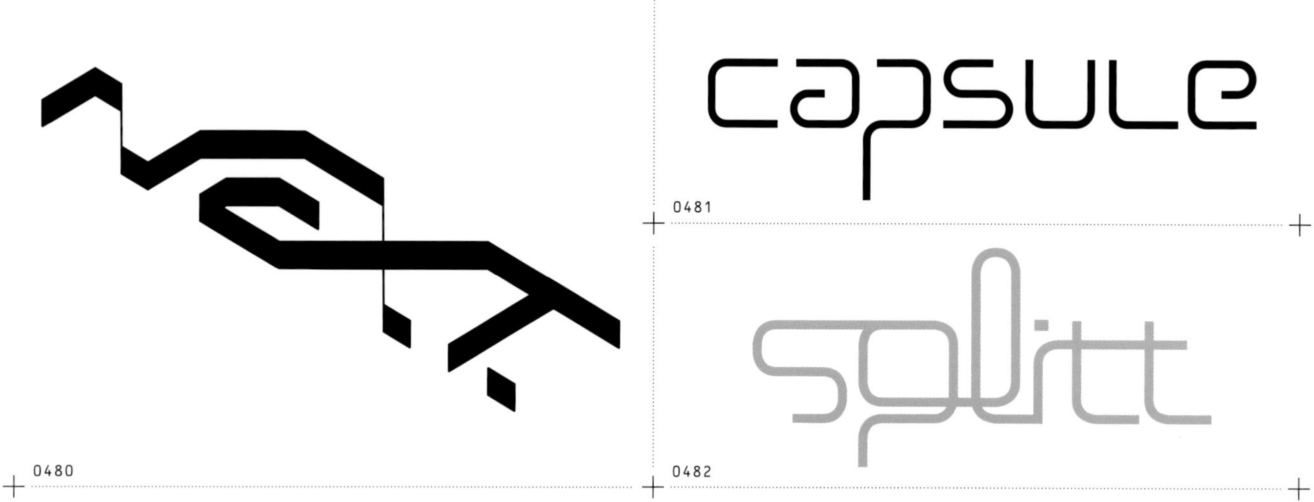

0480

0481

0482

Heroes' Connection

0483

0484

0485

0486

0487

0488

0489

0490

0491

clickmusic.jp

0492

0493

0494

0495

0496

0497

0498

0499

0500

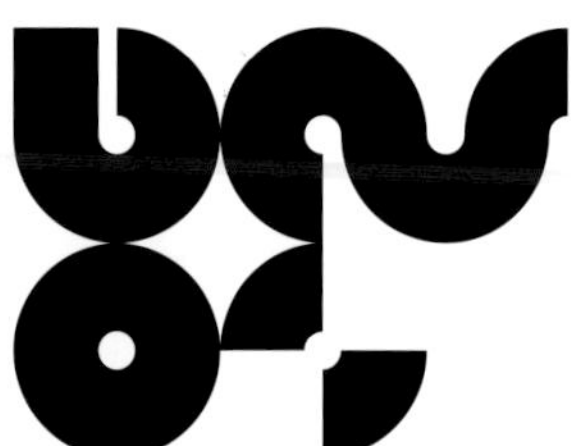

0501

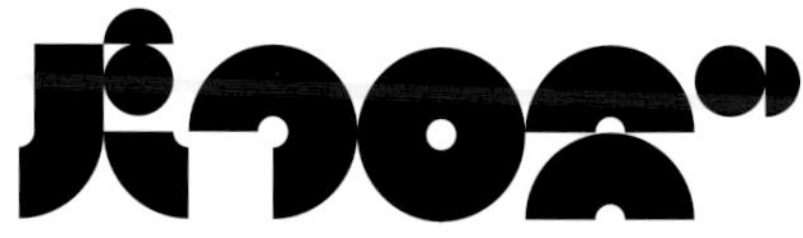

0502

0503

0504

0505

0506

0507

0508

0509

0510

0511

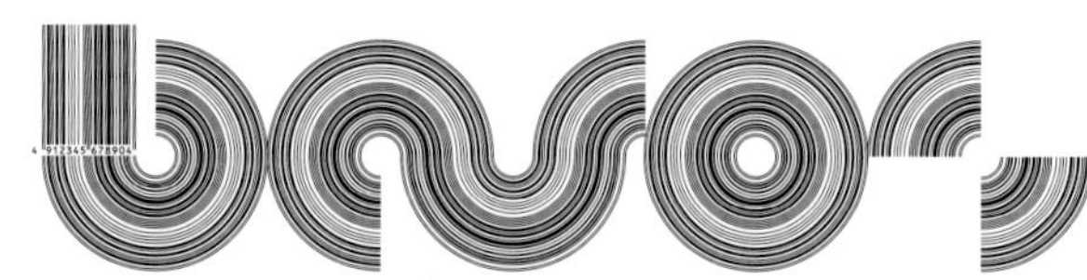

0512

0513

deadline

0514

0515

0516

0517

0518

0519

0520

0521

0522

0523

0524

0525

0526

0527

0528

0529

0530

0531

0532

AdDicTed to Ride

0533

0534

0535

0536

0537

head way

0538

555 [DESIGN]

0539

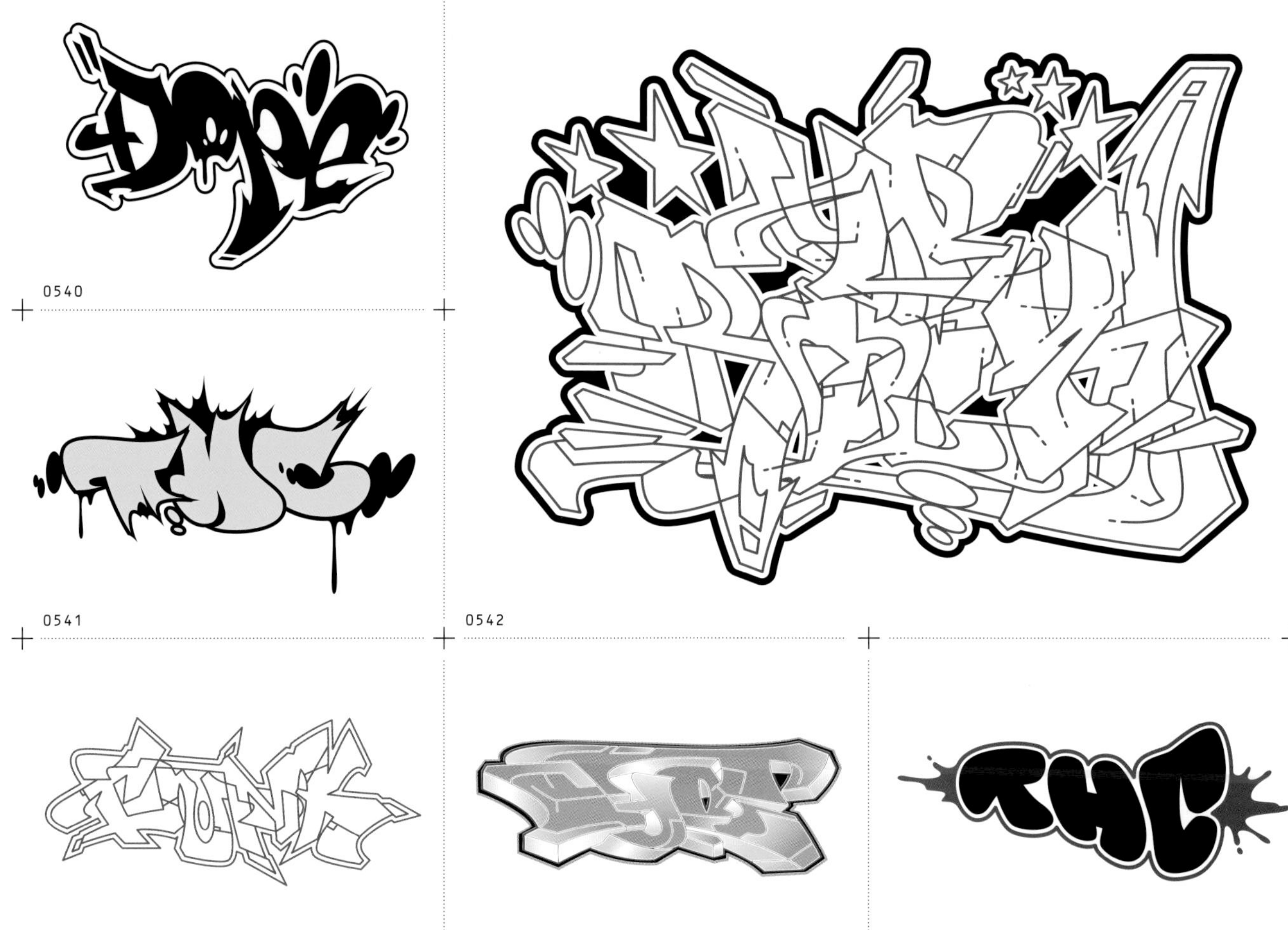

0540

0541

0542

0543

0544

0545

0546

0547

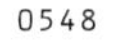

0548

0549

0550

0551

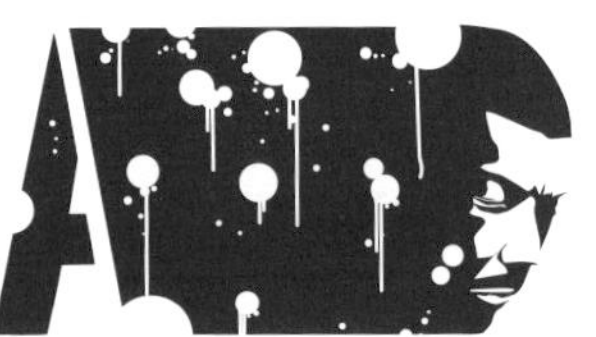

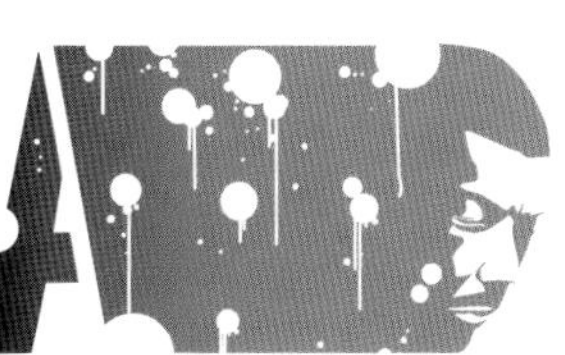

0552

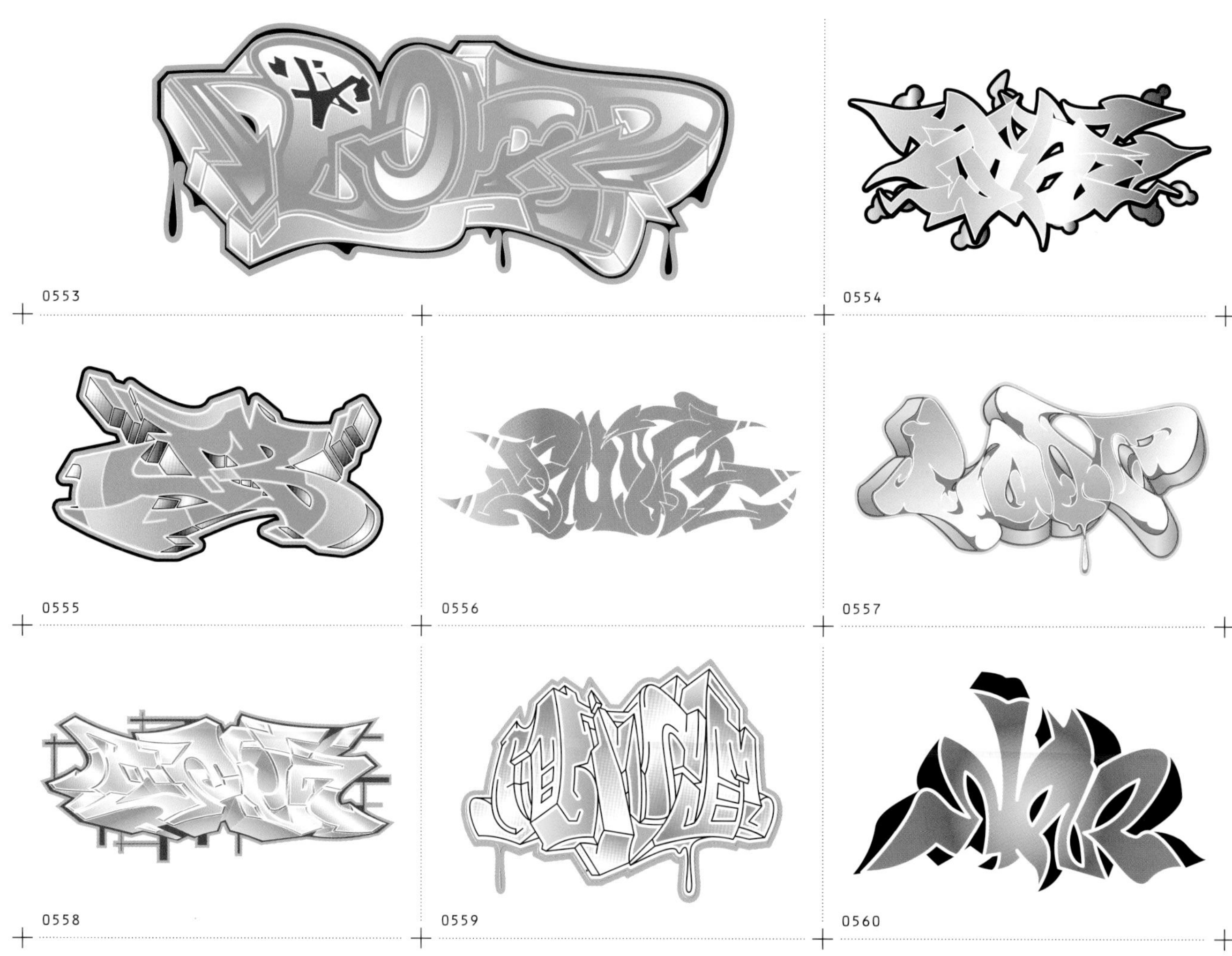

0553

0554

0555

0556

0557

0558

0559

0560

0561

0562

0563

0564

0565

0566

0567

0568

0569

0570

0571

0572

0573

FANTACY

0574

0575

0576

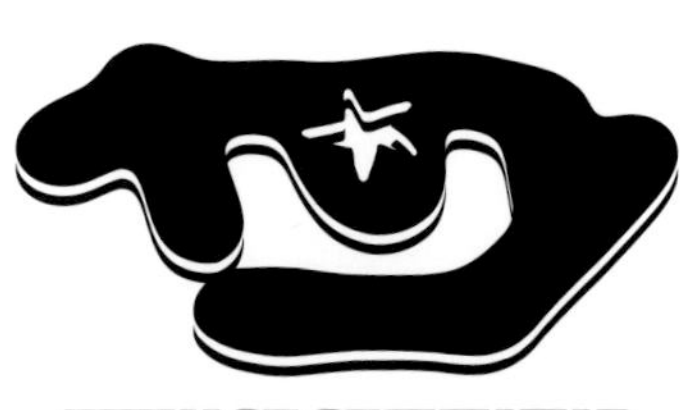

0577

0578

0579

0580

0581

0582

0583

THE SCREAM OF MADNESS

0584

0585

0586

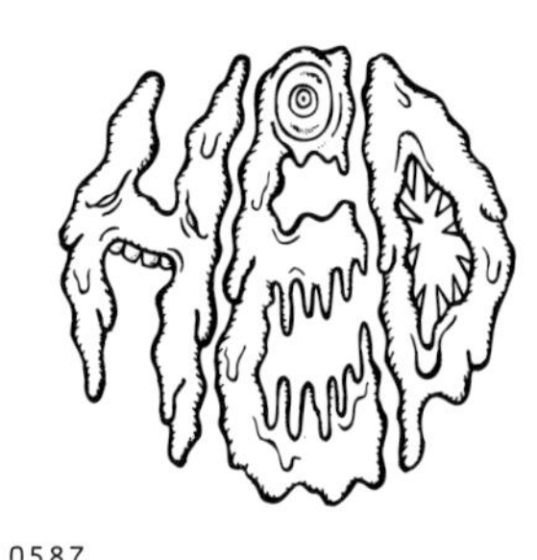

0587

0588

0589

0590

0591

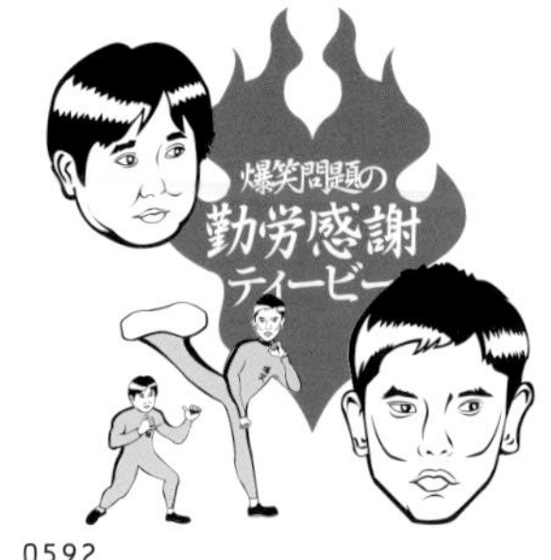

0592

0593

0594

0595

0596

0597

0598

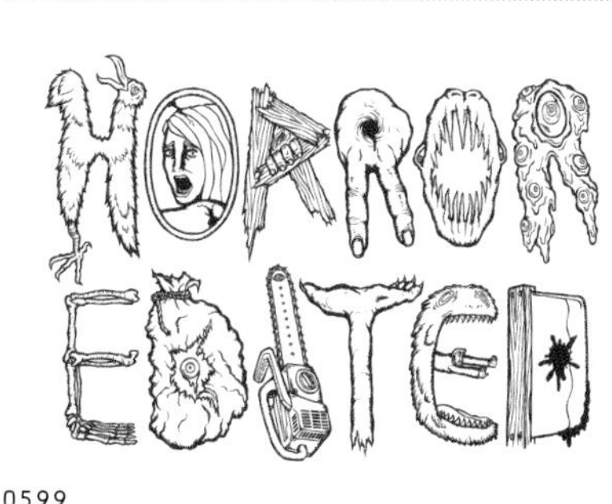

0599

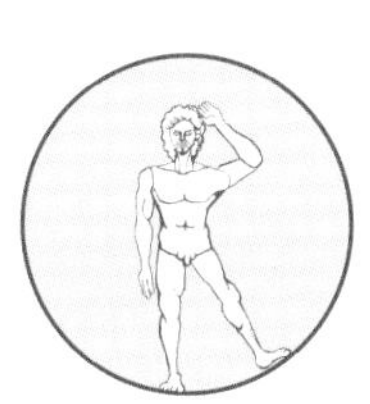

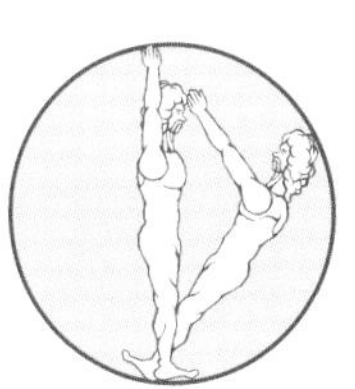
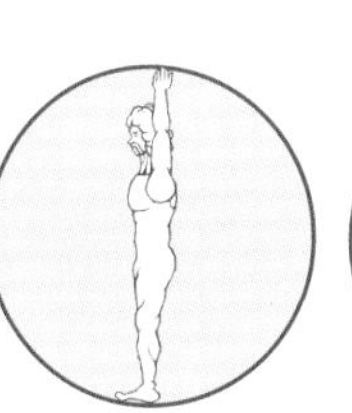

0600

0601

0602

0603

DR GONZO

0604

eight café

0605

ไม่มีอะไรเลย

0606

0607

Final total Eclipse of the millennium

0608

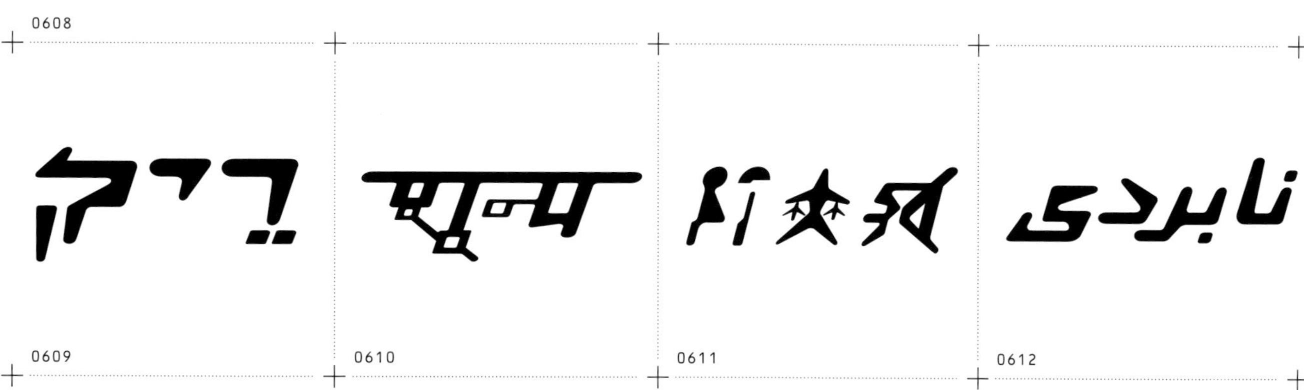

0609

0610

0611

0612

0613

0614

réMan FAmiLial

0615

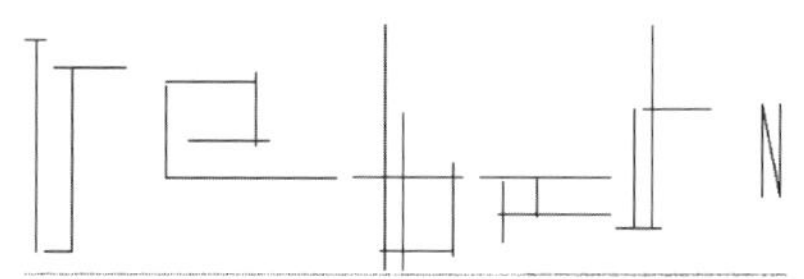

0616

0617

Tridia.

0618

0619

0620

0621

0622

0623

0624

0625

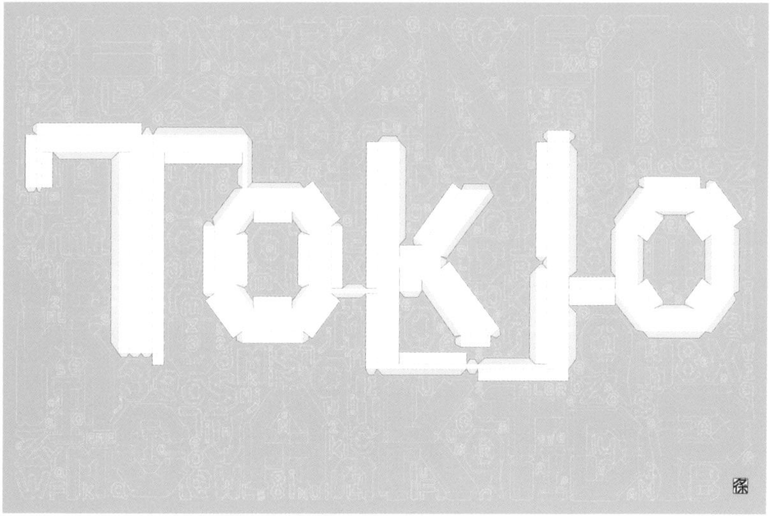

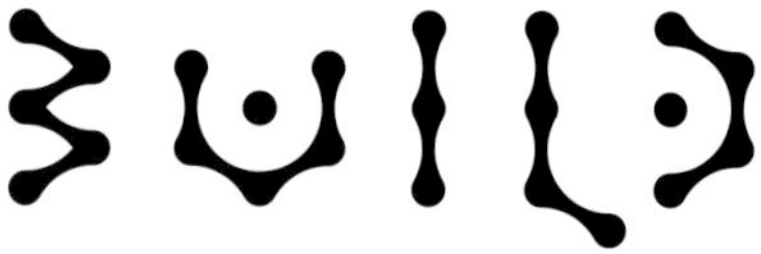

Tokyo

0626

build

0627

R.O.M.

0628

obscure Language

0629

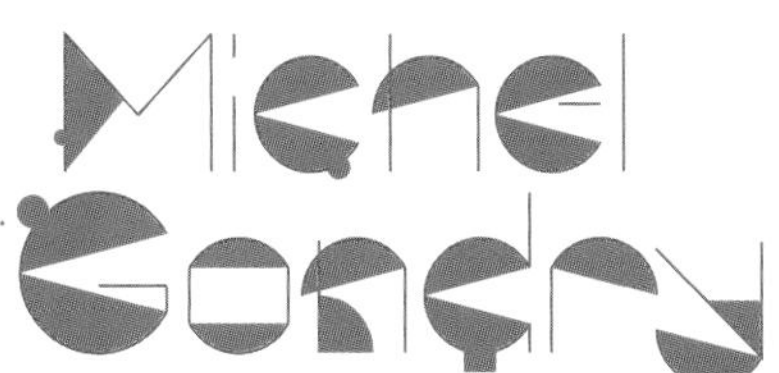

0630

0631

0632

0633

0634

0635

0636

0637

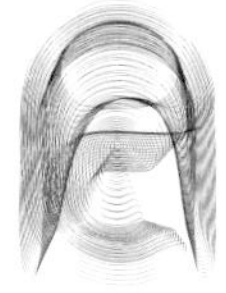

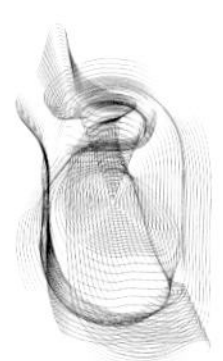
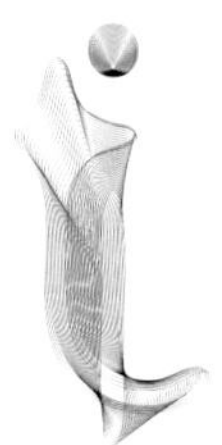

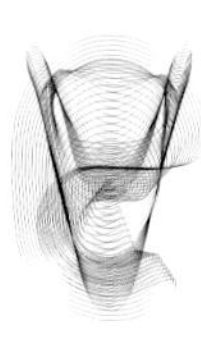

0638

0639

0640

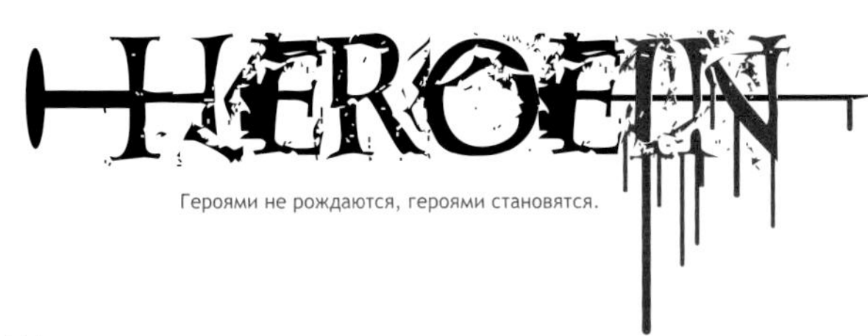

0641

0642

echelon

0643

0644

jetfilm

0645

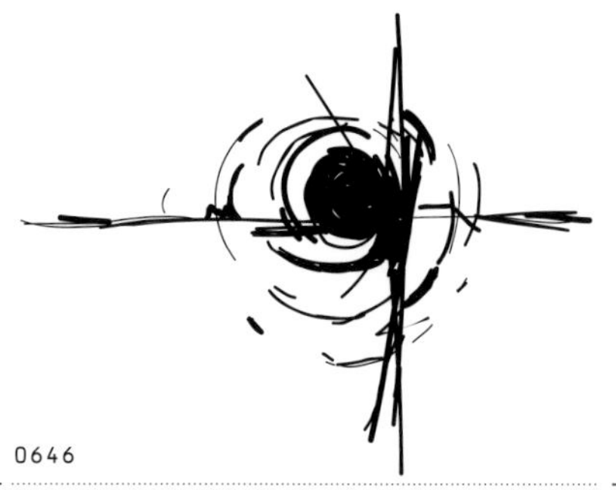

0646

0647

0648

Museum
für Angewandte Kunst
Frankfurt

0649

0650

Good Tuning

0651

0652

0653

0654

0655

Space Shower Digital Archives X

0656

0657

Kitchen

0658

teenage 3 of the year

0659

0660

0661

0662

0663

0664

0666

0665

0667

0668

0669

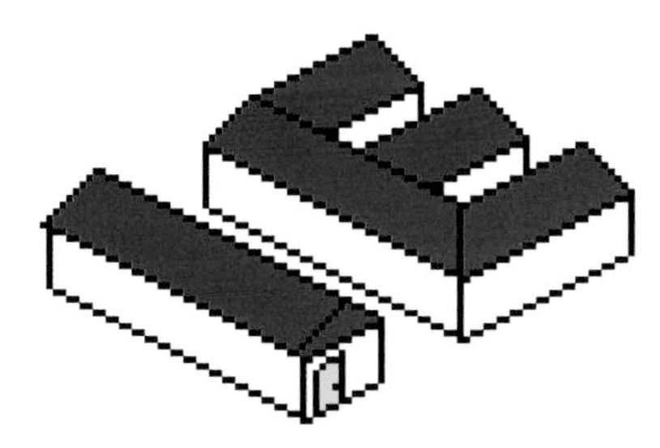

0670

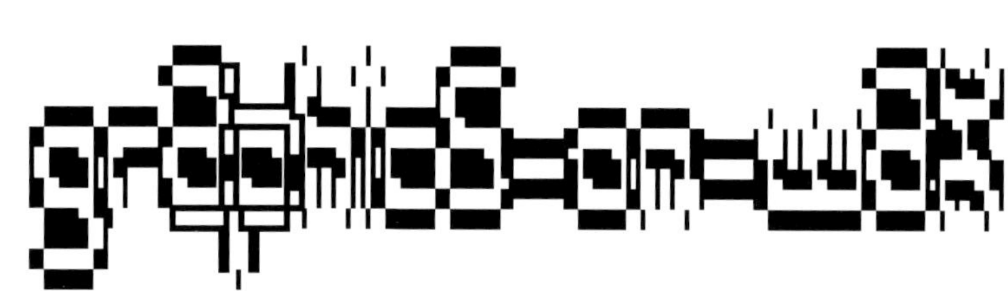

0671

0672

0673

0674

0675

0676

0677

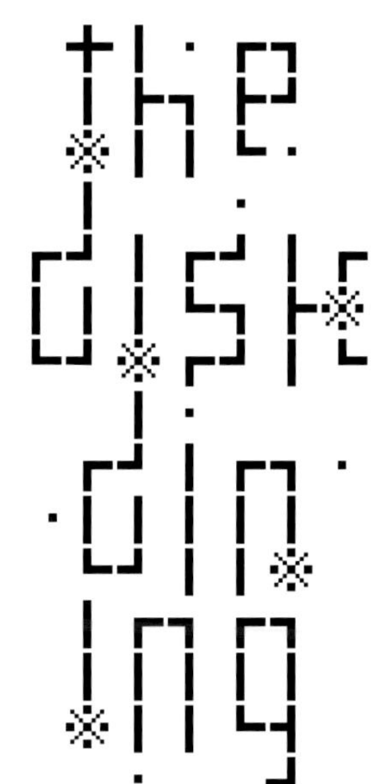

0678

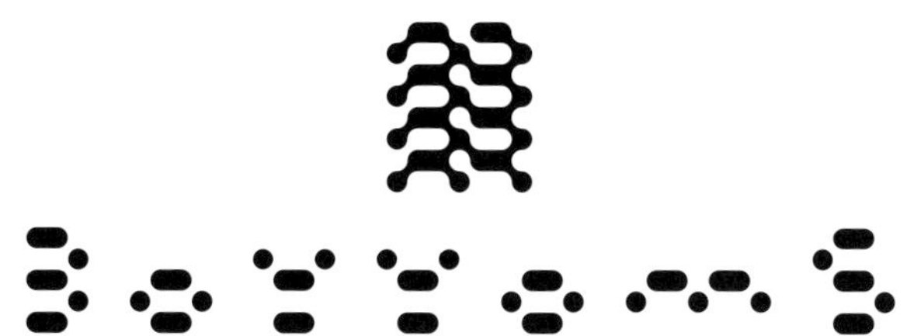

0679

0680

NUIT
BLANCHE

0681

0682

0683

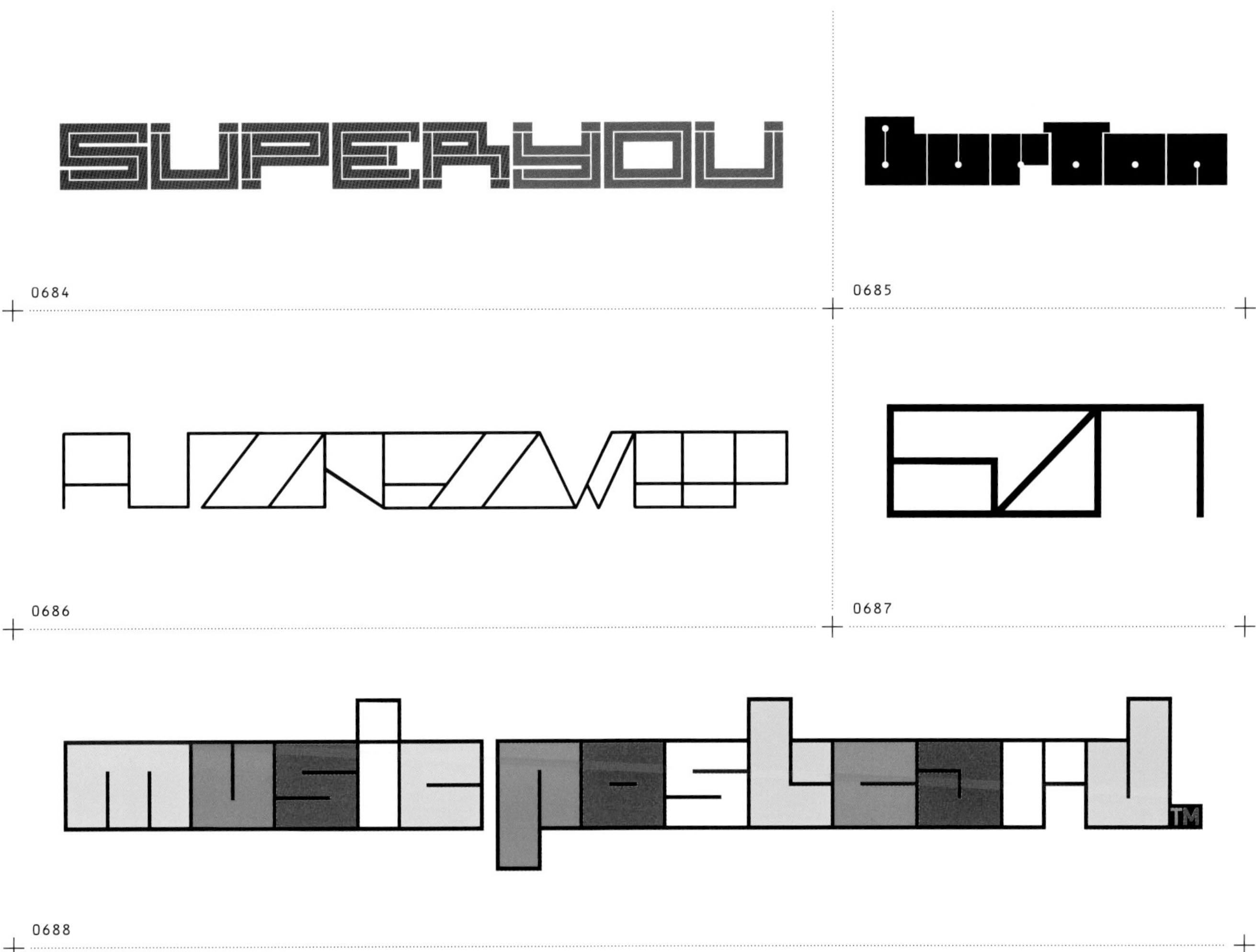

0684

0685

0686

0687

0688

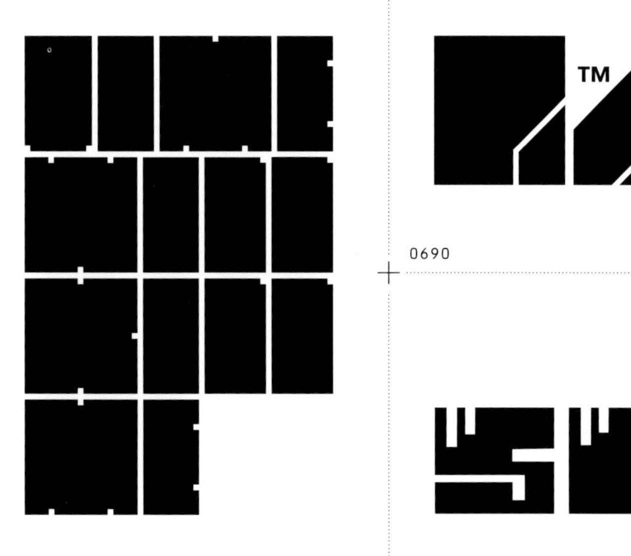

0689

0690

0691

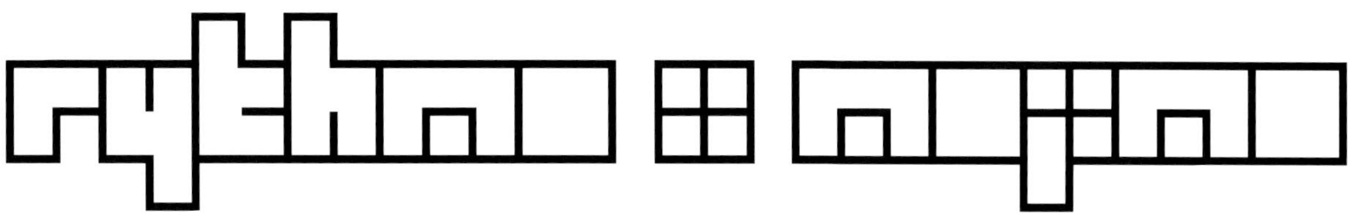

0692

0693

0694

0695

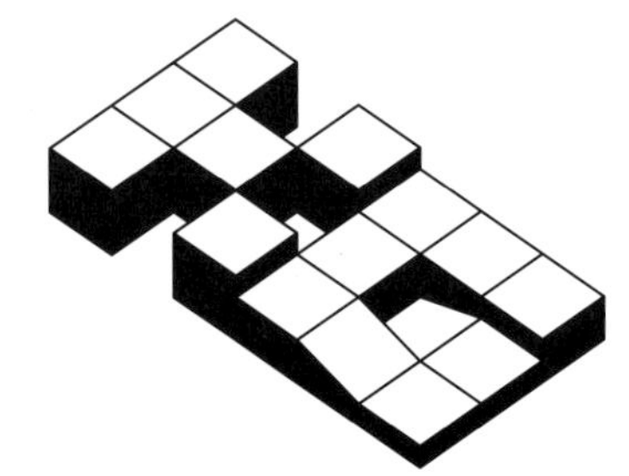

0696

0697

0698

0699

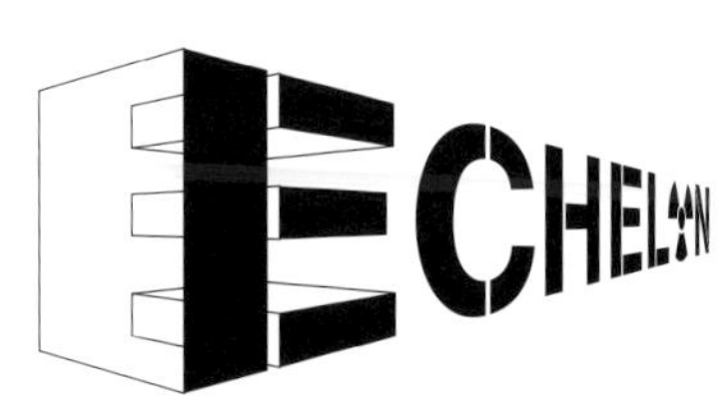

0700

0701

0702

0703

0704

ELECTRICS
CAN BE REPRODUCED WITHOUT LIMIT.

0705

0706

MOVE

0707

0708

0709

0710

0711

0712

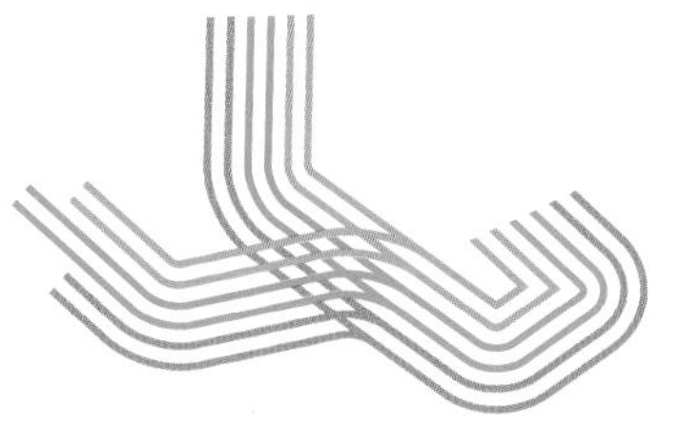

0713

haus Zauberberg

0714

0715

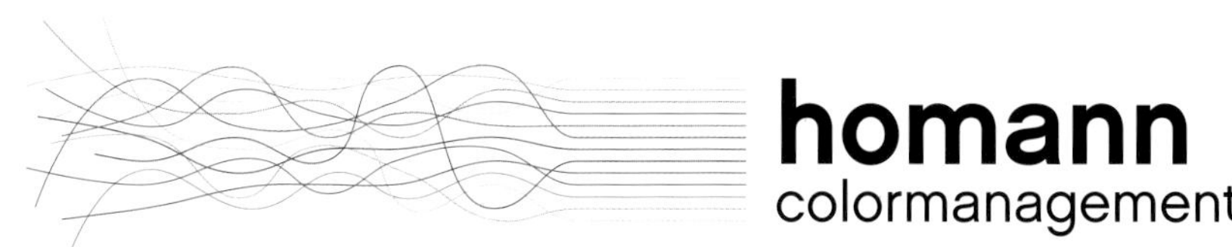

0716

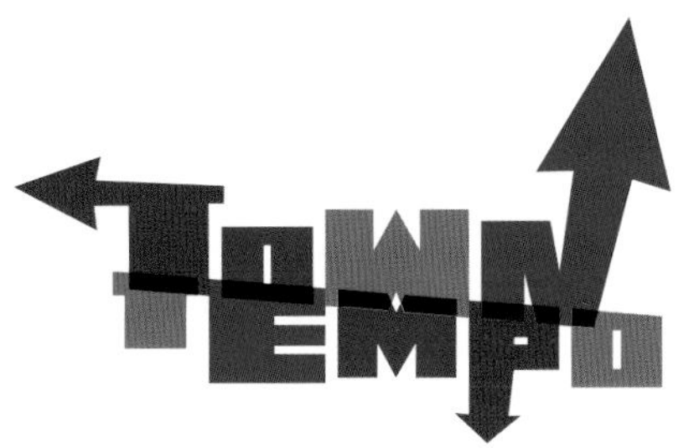

0717

Re 96

96 Re 06

0718

0719

0721

0722

0720

0723

Notsuperstitious records

0724

0725

0726

0727

0728

0729

0730

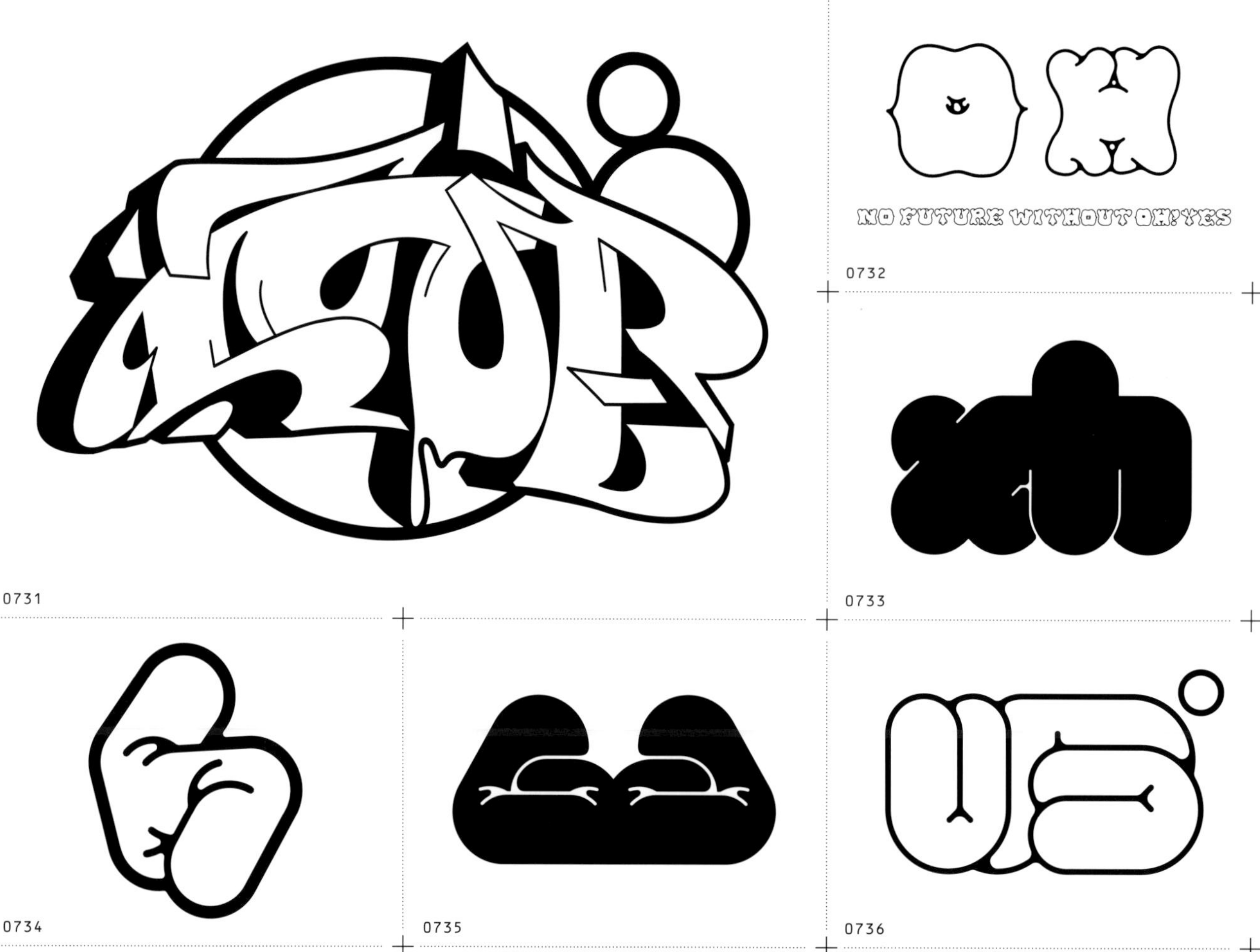

0731

0732

0733

0734

0735

0736

0737

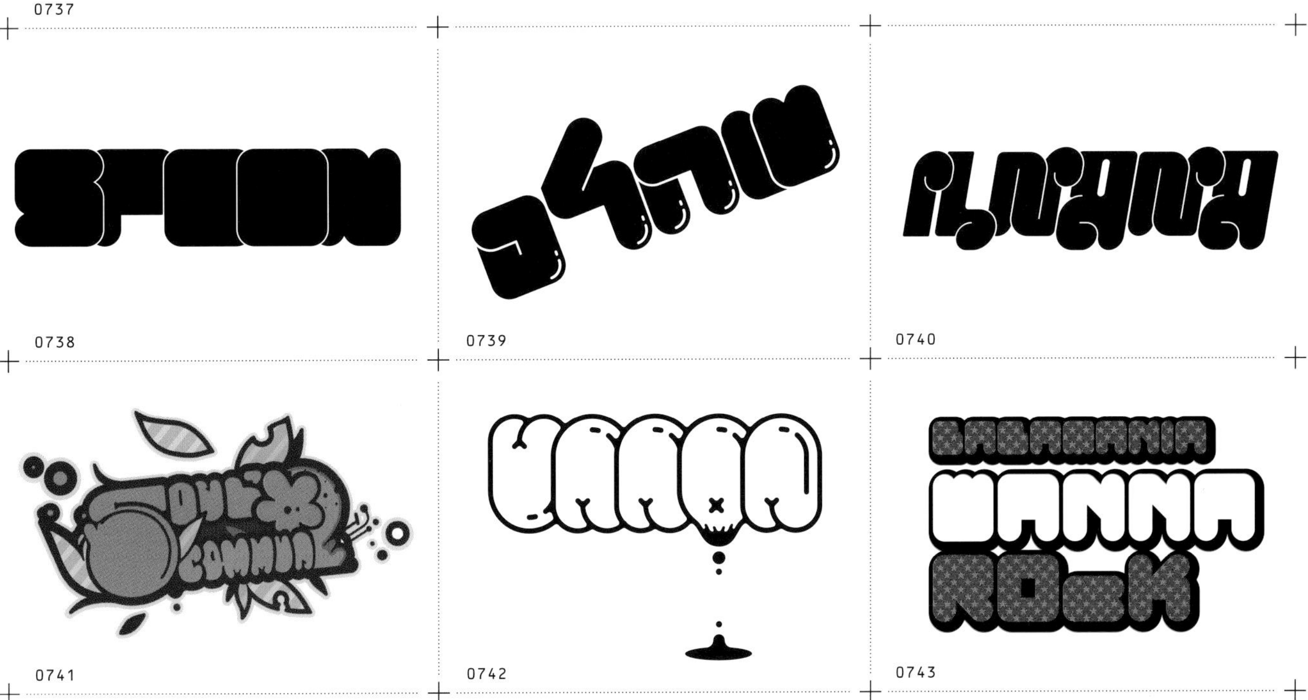

0738

0739

0740

0741

0742

0743

0744

0745

0746

0747

KISS

0748

BURTON

0749

FUX

0750

0751

0752

0753

I want a lot of them for a Utopia

0754

Liquidroom

0755

0756

NOSEtalgia

0757

icon

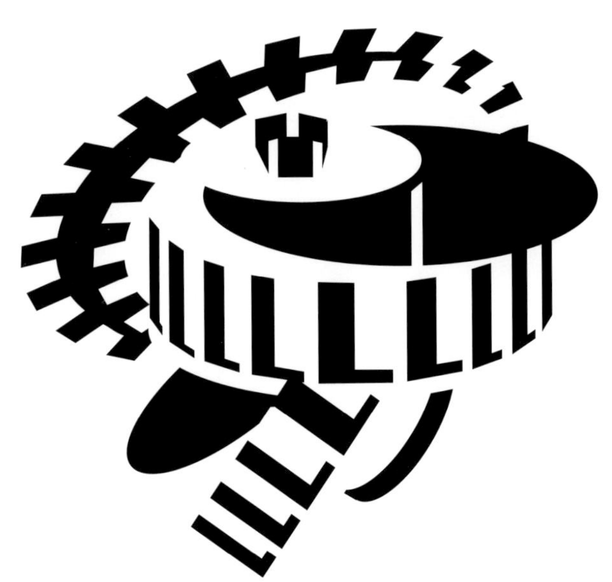

0758

0760

0759

0761

0763

0764

0765

0762

0766

0767

0768

0769

0770

0771

0772

0773

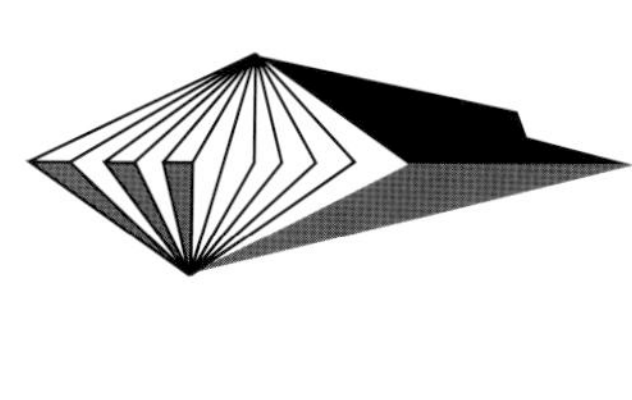

0774

0775

0776

0777

0778

0779

0780

0781

0782

0783

0784

0785

Grizi
Sistem

17.02.2000. Београд
НАРОДНИ
КОНГРЕС
ОТПОР!А

0787

МИСЛИ
ПРУЖИ
ОТПОР!
www.otpor.com

0788

0789

0790

0791

ОТПОР! ЊЕМУ!

НАША МЕТА

0792

ШТА 'ОЋЕШ?

ЈЕБЕНИ
"НОВИ МИЛЕНИЈУМ"
ИЛИ
УСРАНИ
СРЕДЊИ ВЕК

ОТПОР!

0793

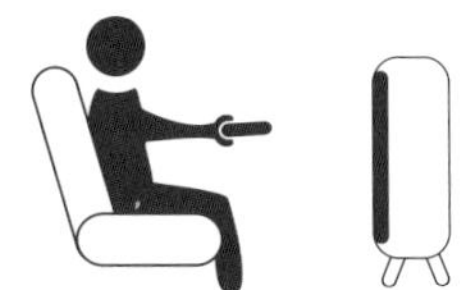

THE LAZY PEOPLE

0794

0795

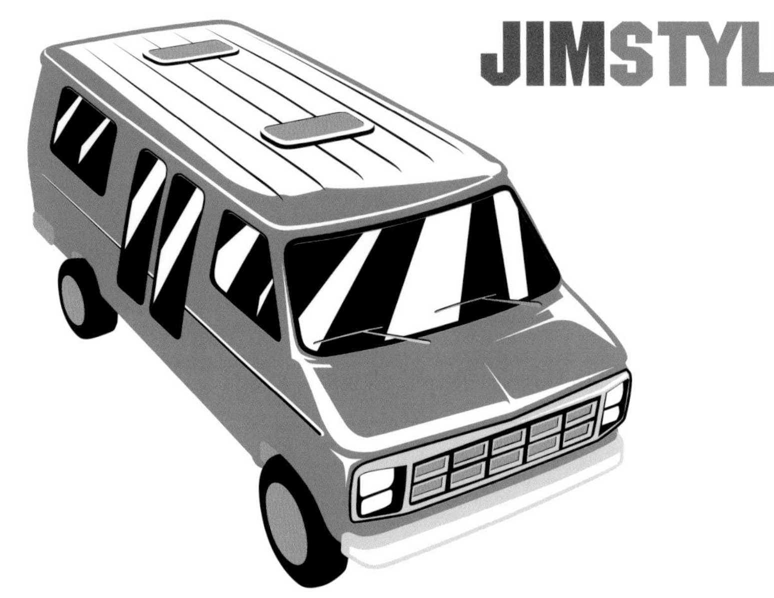

0796

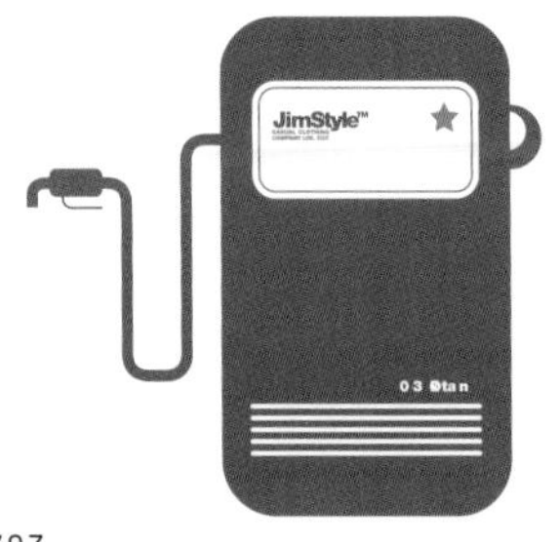

0797

0798

0799

0800

0801

0802

0803

0804

0805

0806

0807

0808

0809

0810

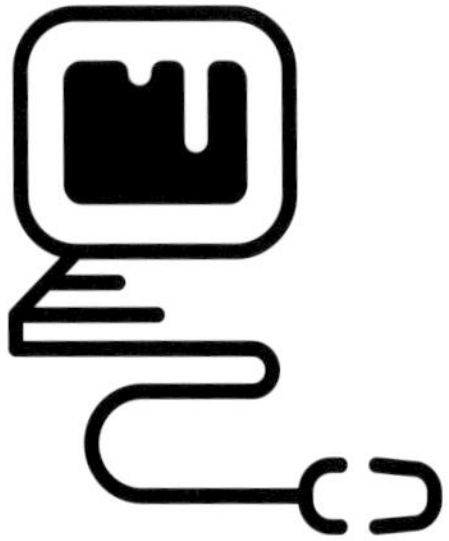

0811

0812

0813

0814

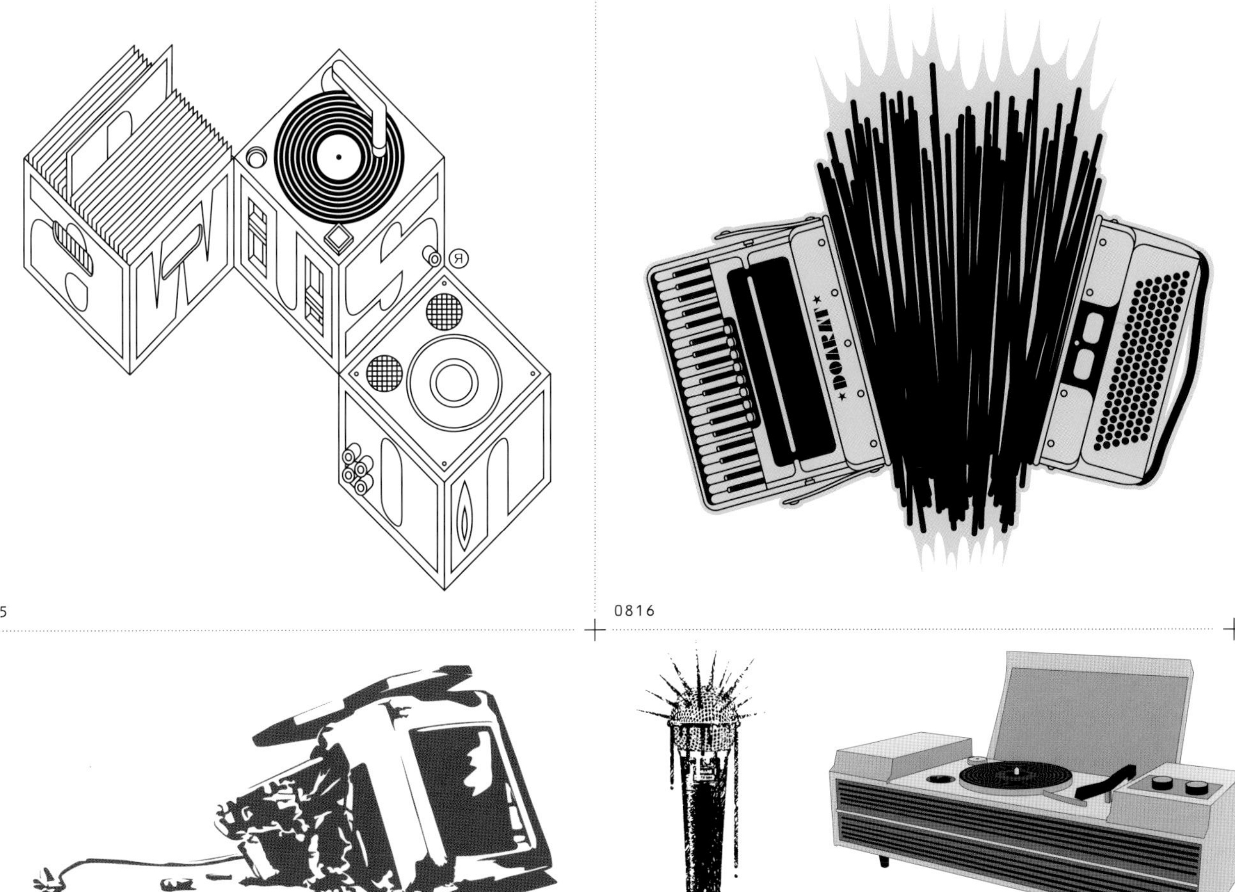

0815

0816

0817

0818

0819

time

e-data

world-t

world-t

0820

culculator

world-t

phone

world-t

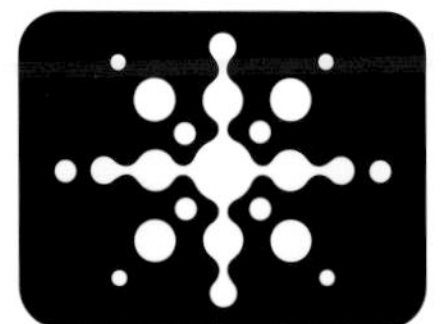
alarm

timer

stop-w

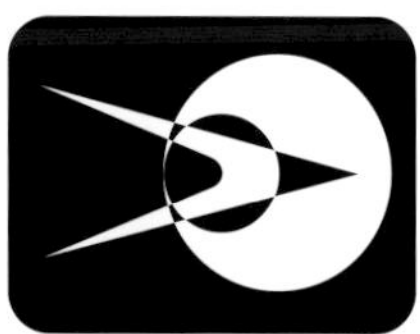
world-t

0821

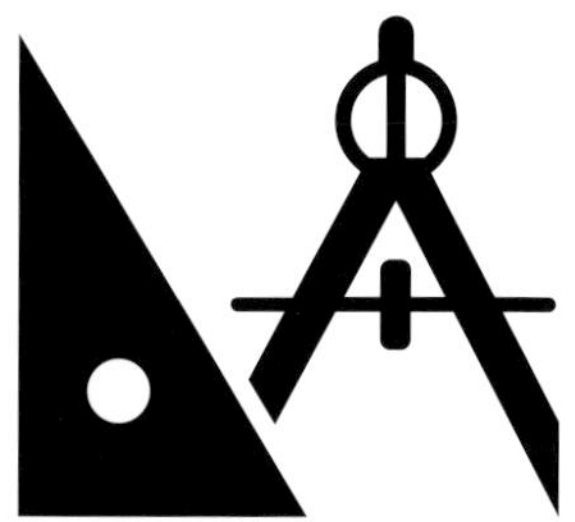

0822

0823

0824

0825

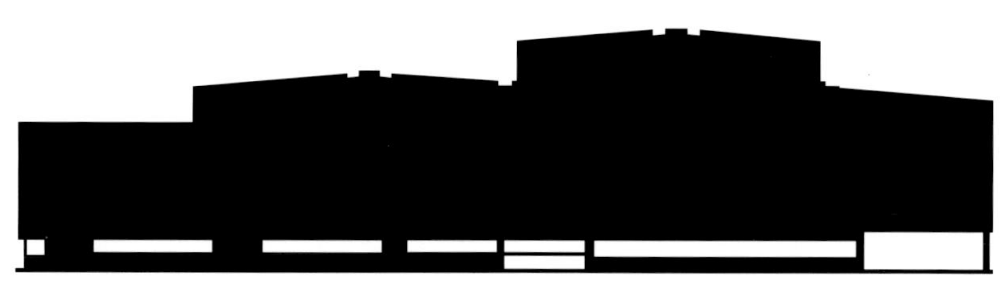

0826

0827

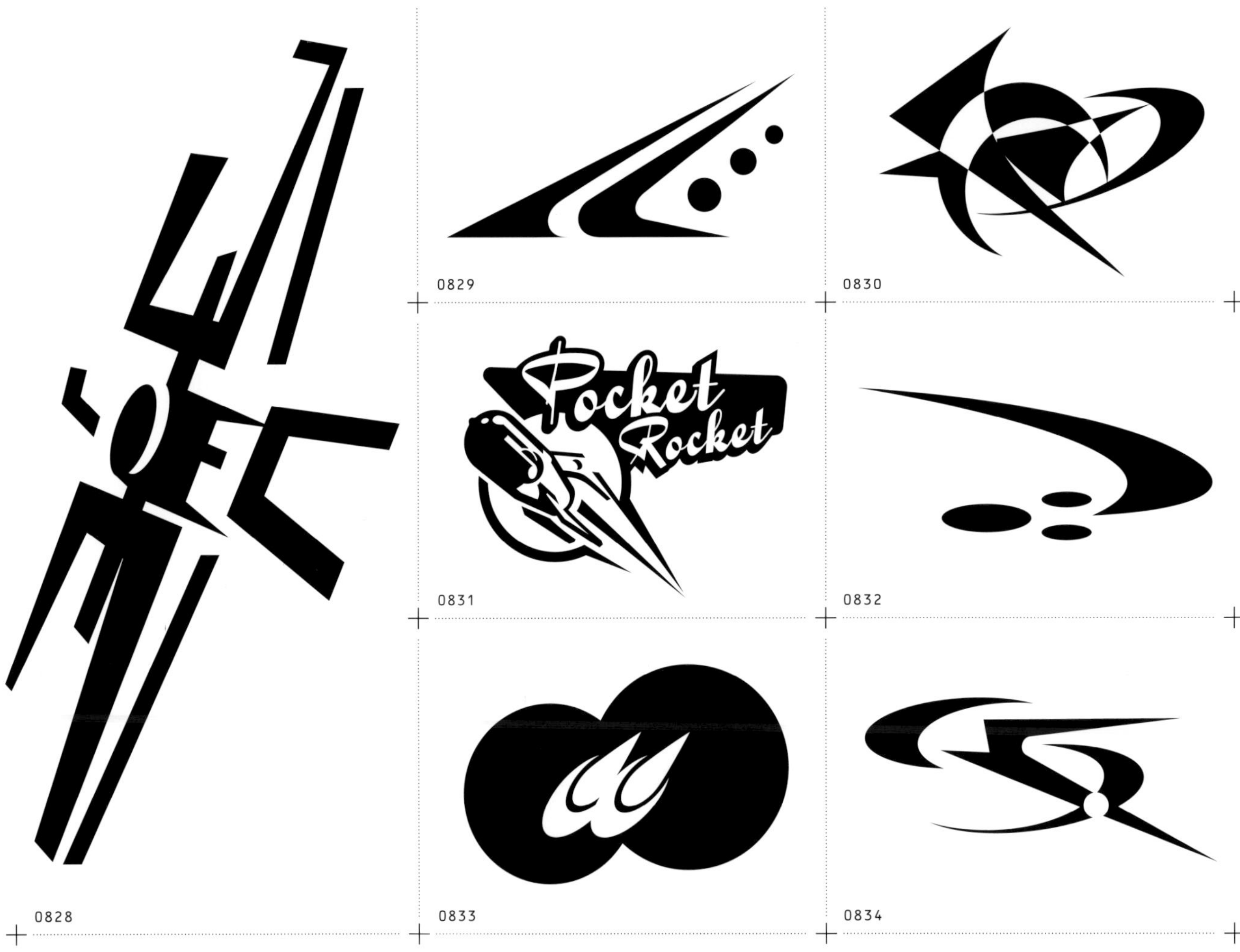

0829 0830 0831 0832 0833 0834 0828

0835

0836

0837

0838

0839

0840

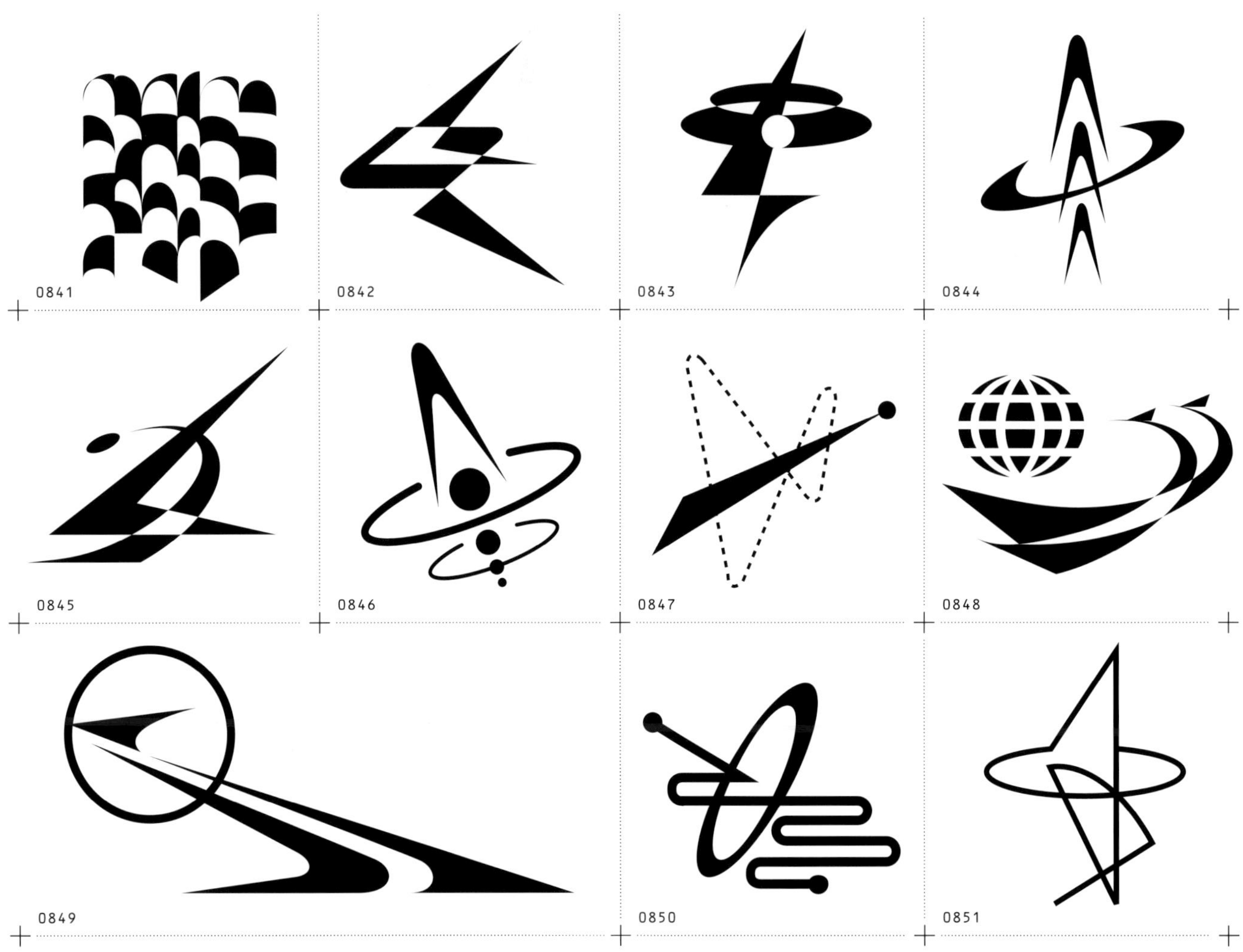
0841
0842
0843
0844
0845
0846
0847
0848
0849
0850
0851

0852

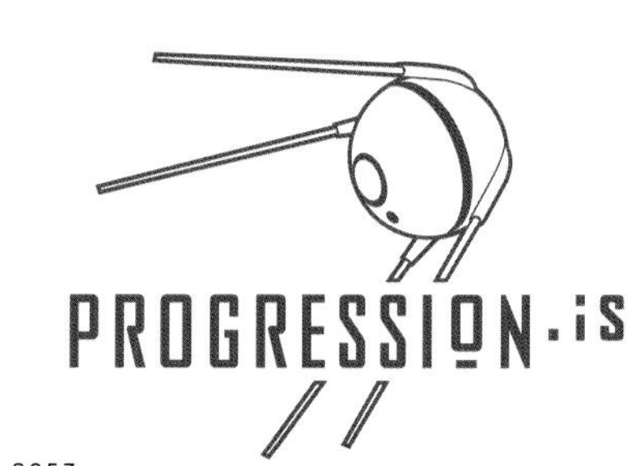

0853

0854

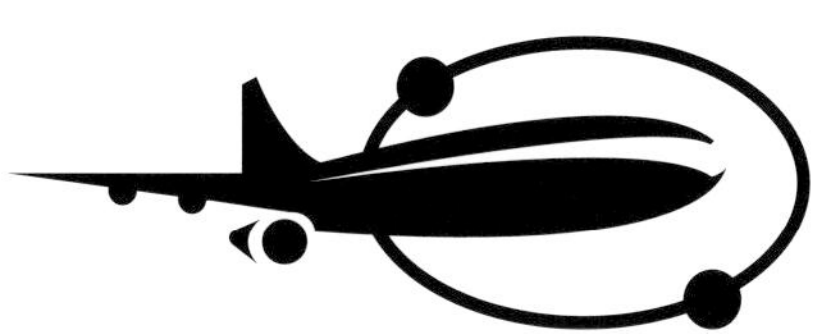

0855

0856

0857

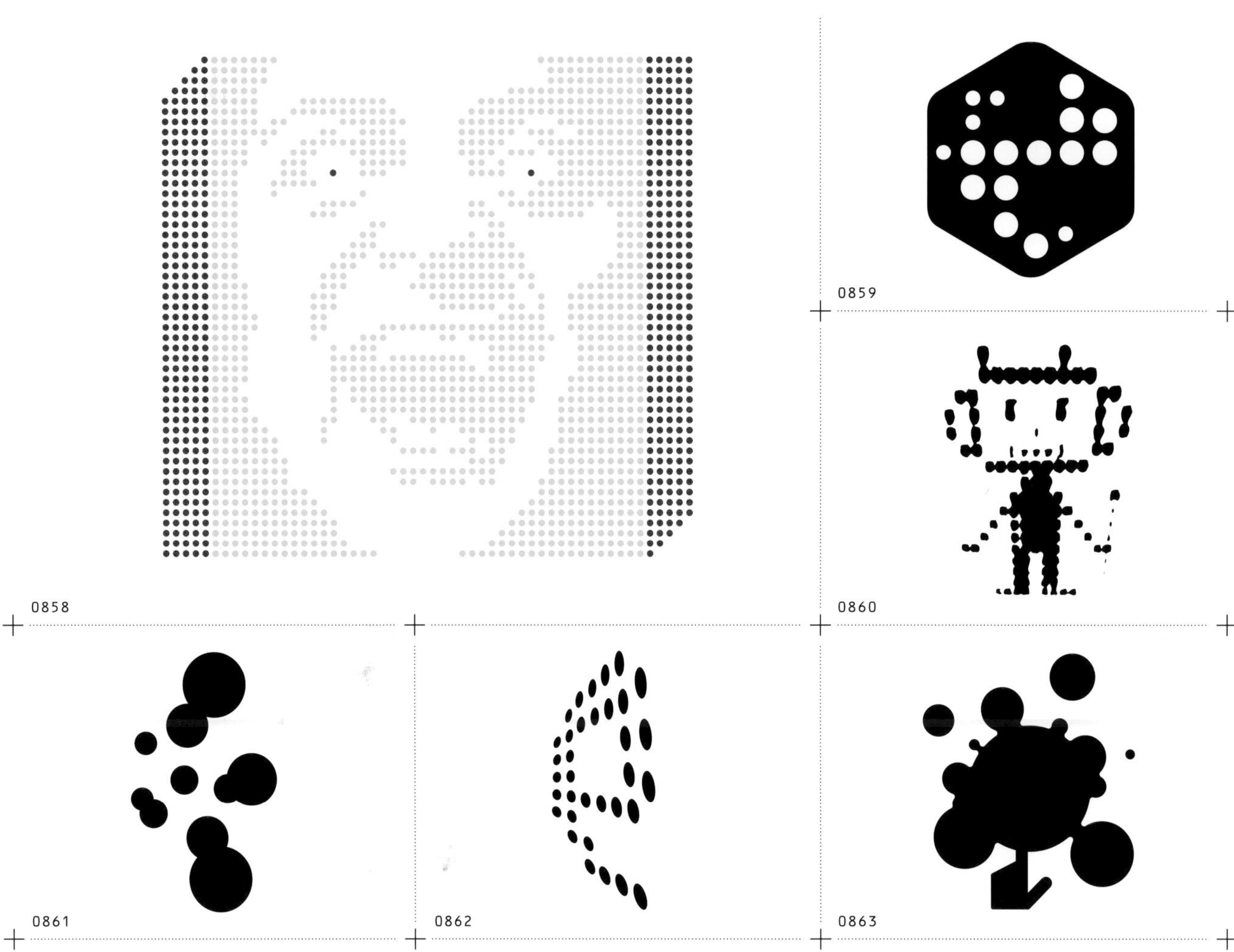

0858

0859

0860

0861

0862

0863

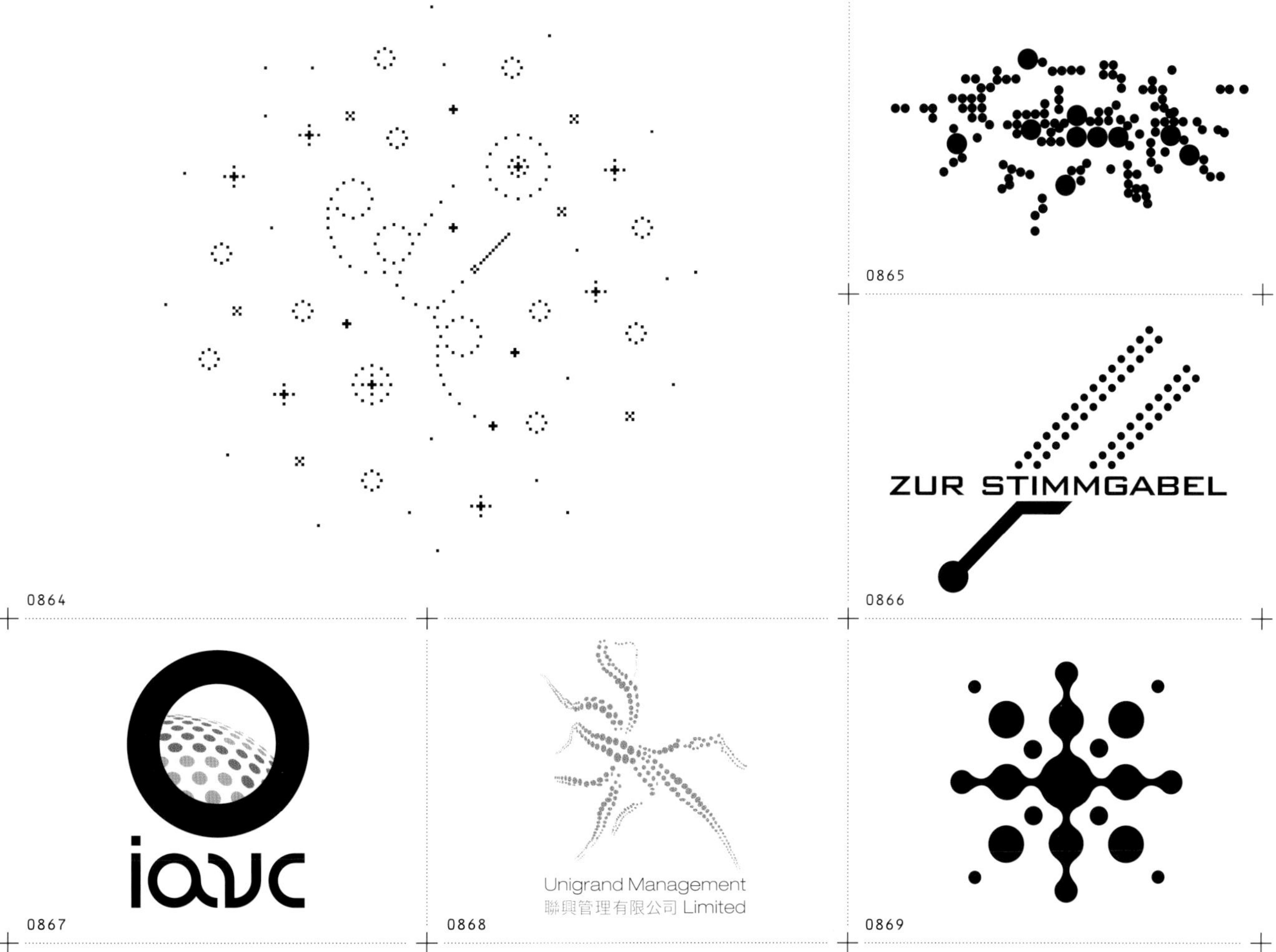

0864

0865

0866

0867

0868

0869

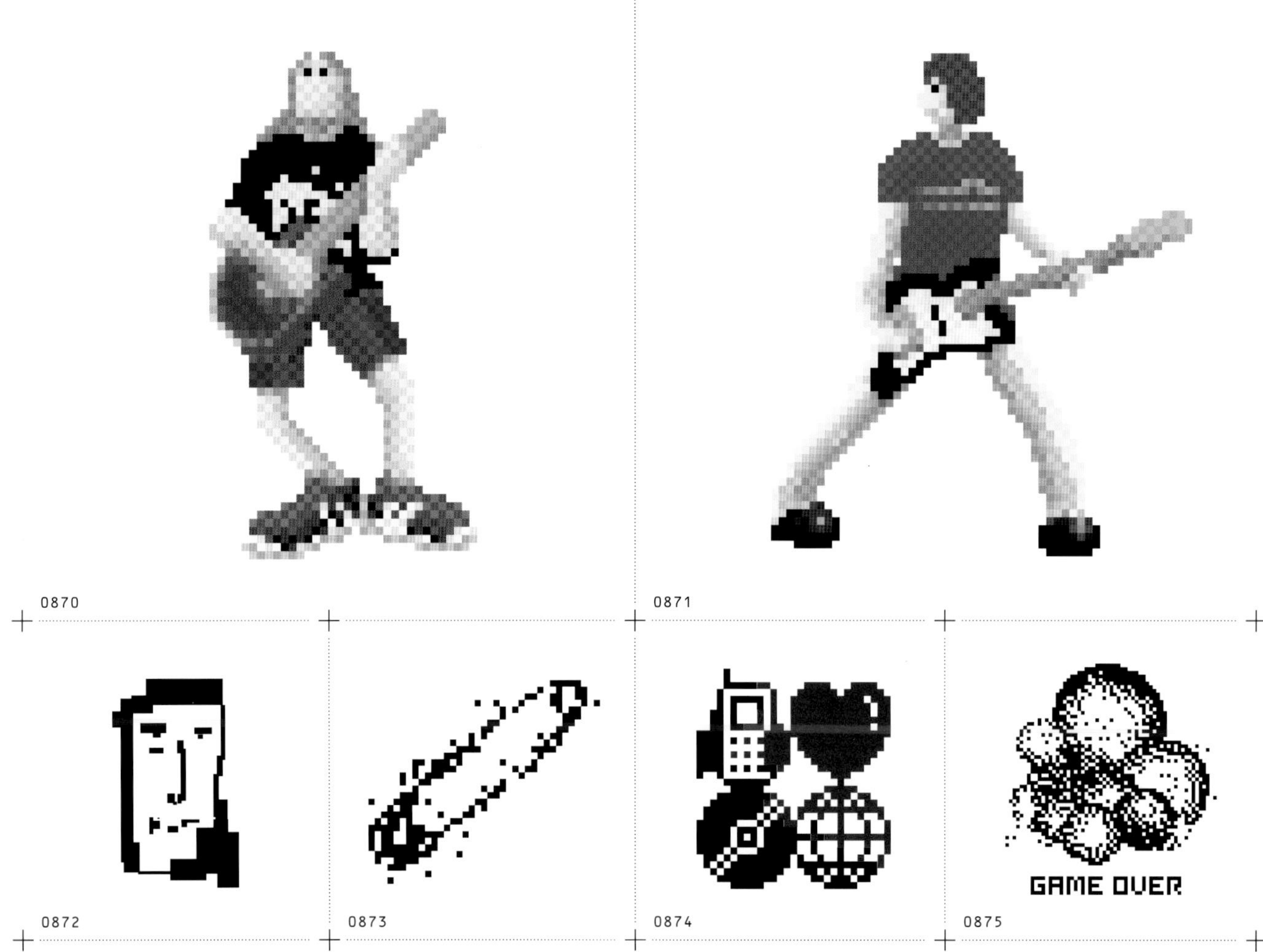

0870 0871

0872 0873 0874 0875

0876

0877

0878

0879

0880

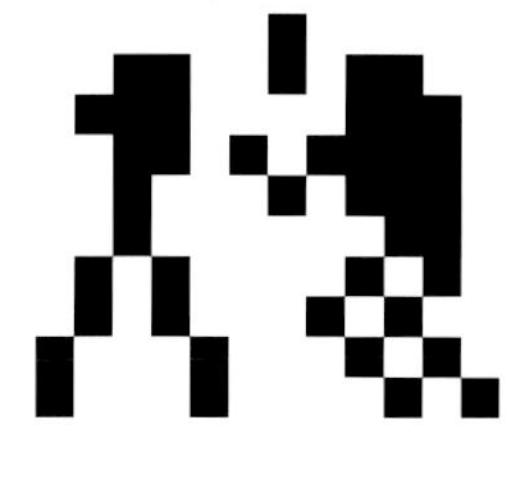

0881

0882

0883

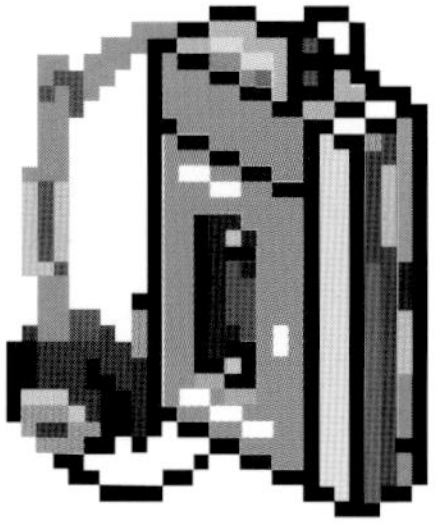

0884

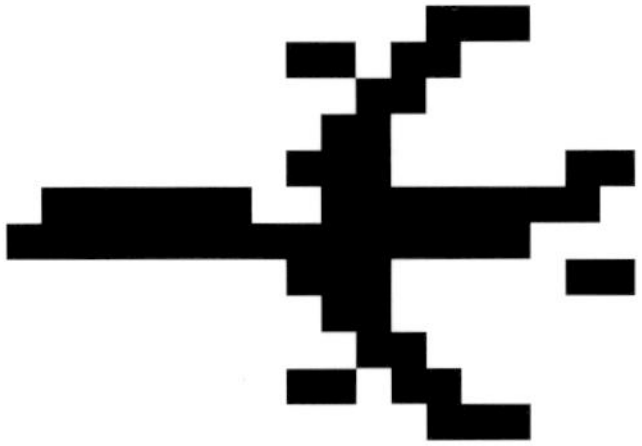

0885

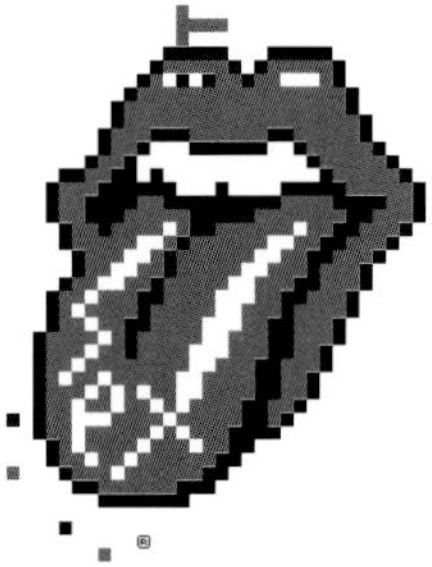

0886

0887

0888

0889

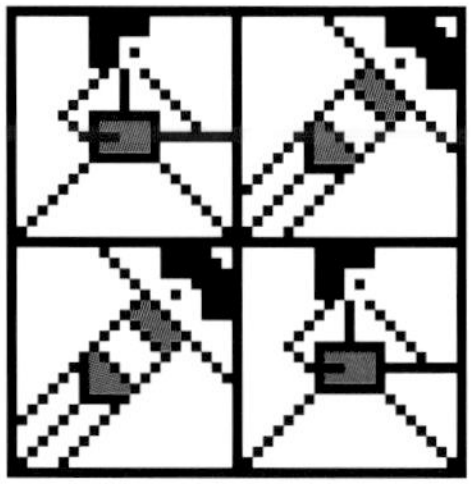

0890

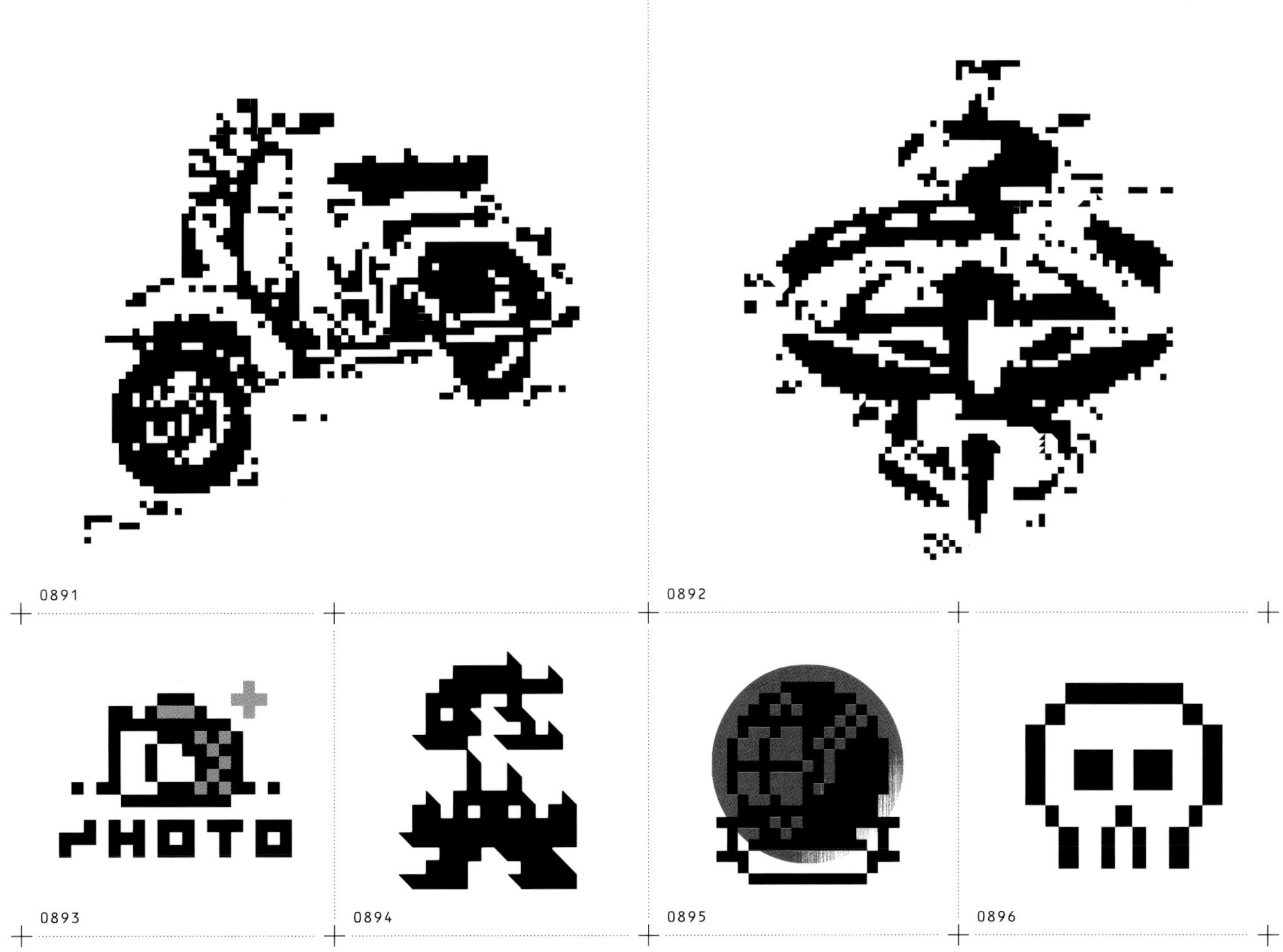

0891

0892

0893

0894

0895

0896

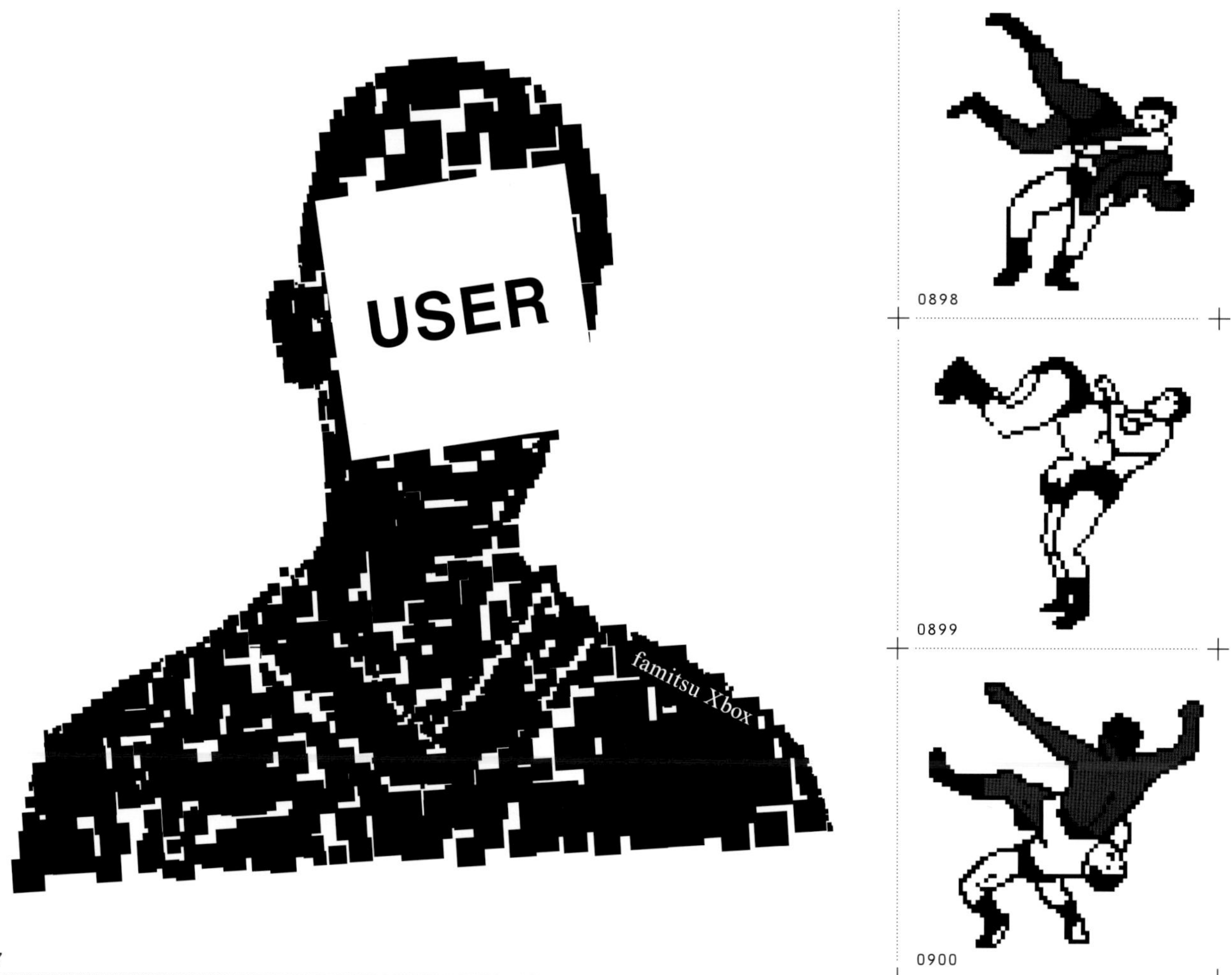

0897

0898

0899

0900

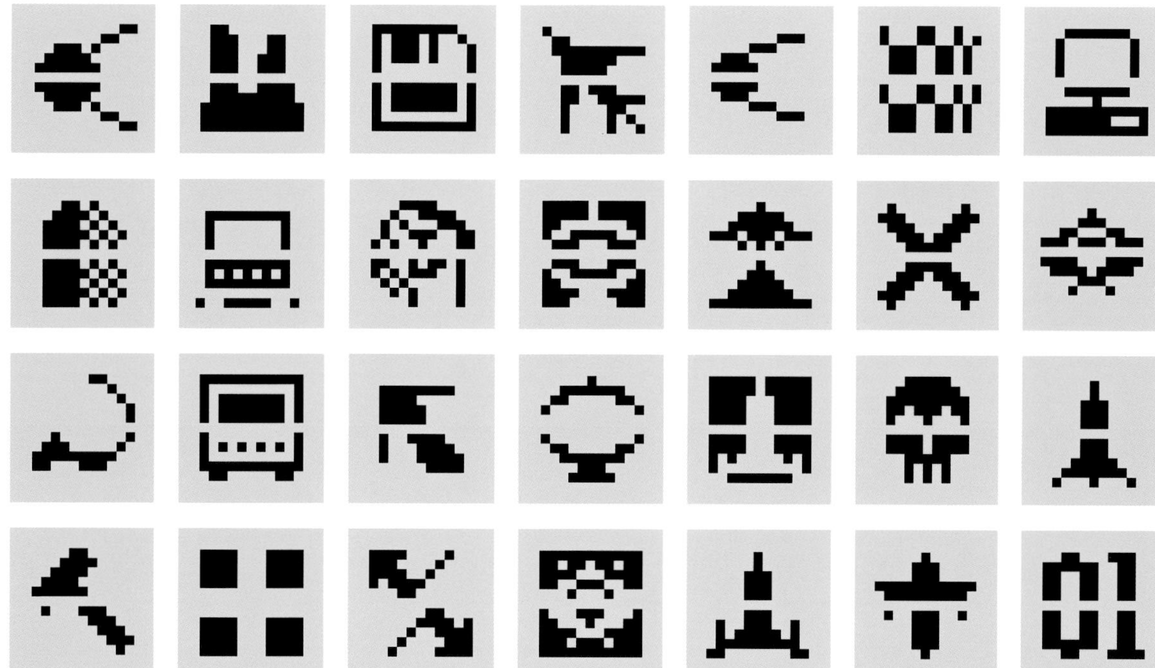

0901

0902

0903

0904

11
30

0905

0906

0907

PLANET®
PIXEL

0908

0909

0910

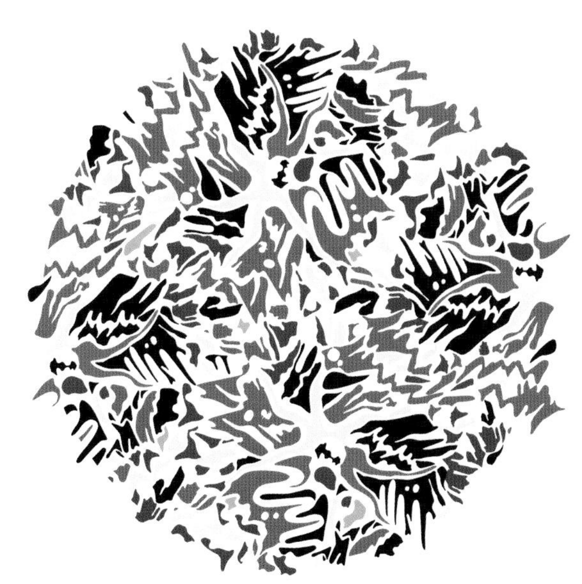

0911

0912

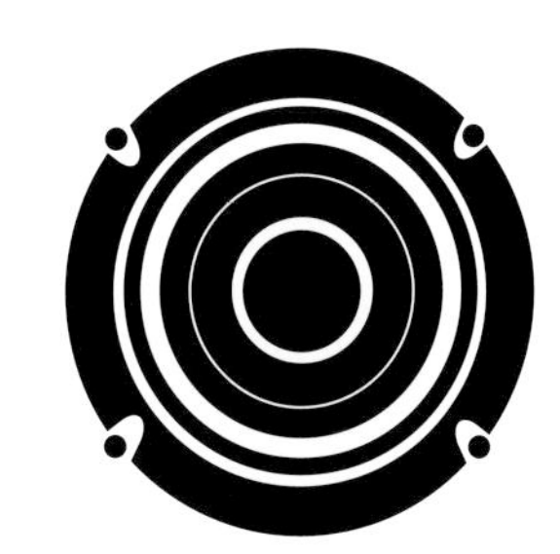

0913

0914

0915

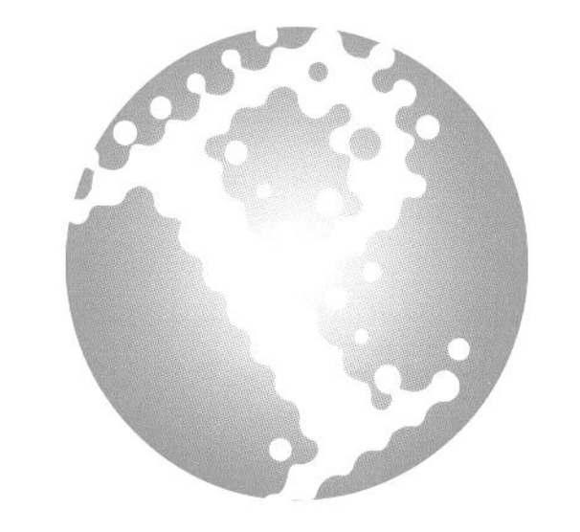

0916

0917

0918

0919

0920

0921

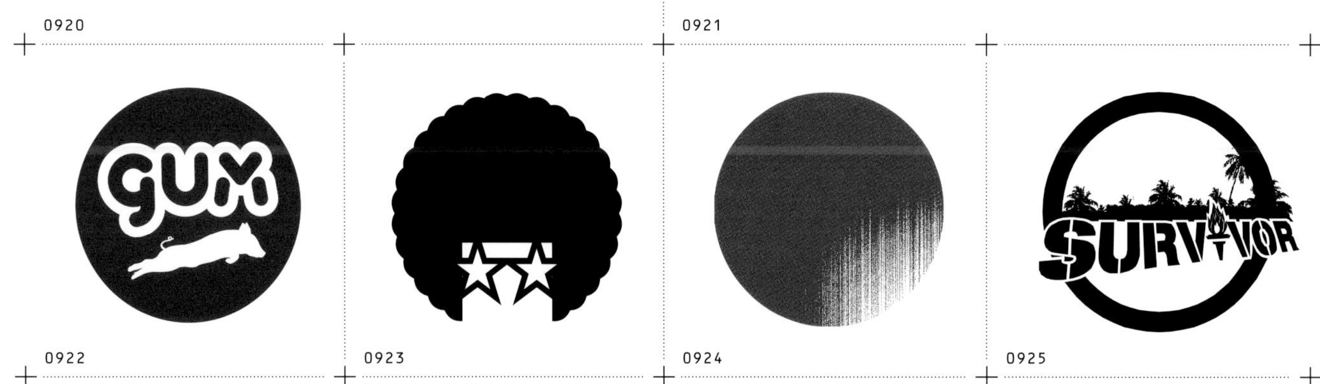

0922

0923

0924

0925

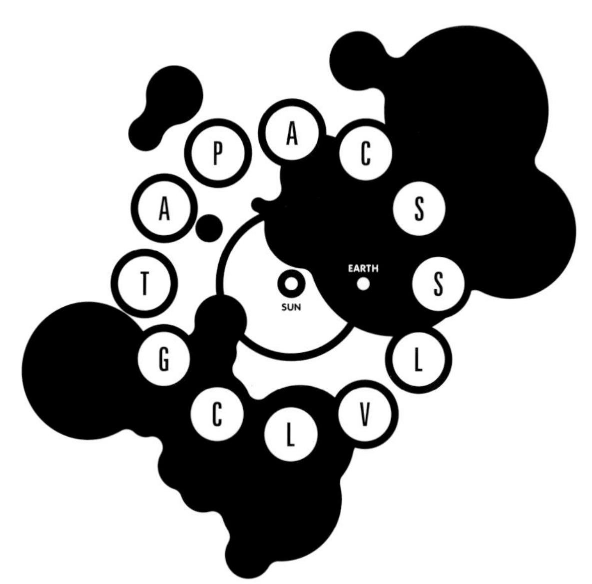

0926

0927

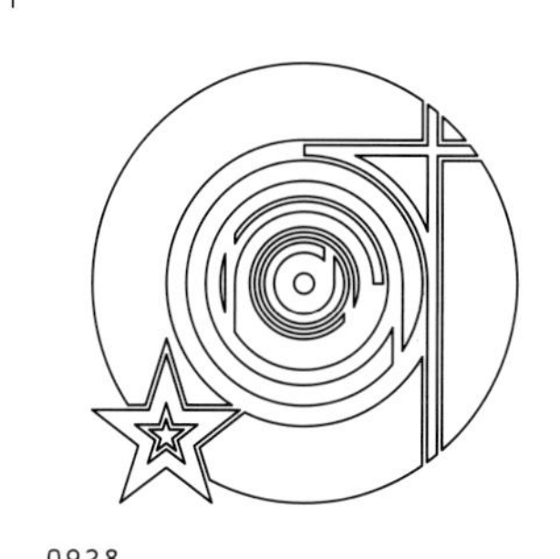

0928

0929

0930

0931

0932

0933

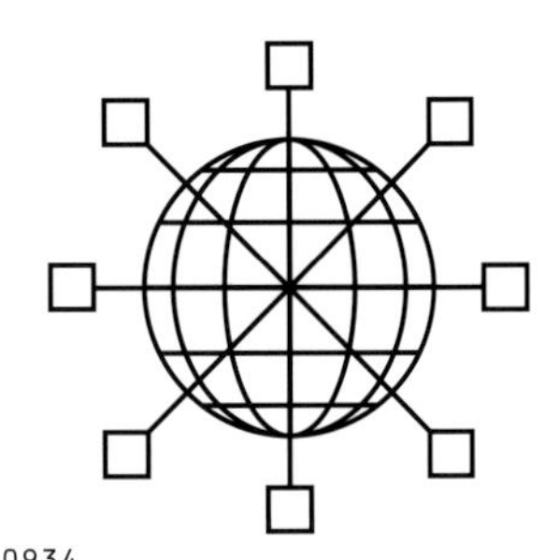

0934

0935

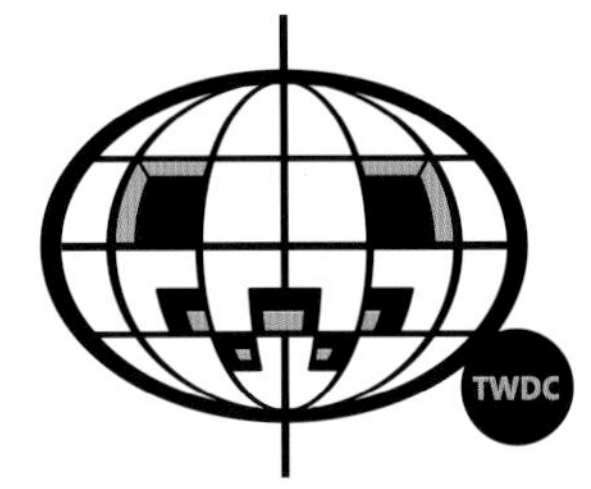

0936

0937

0938

0939

0940

0941

0942

0943

0944

0945

0946

0947

0948

0949

0950

0951

0952

0953

0954

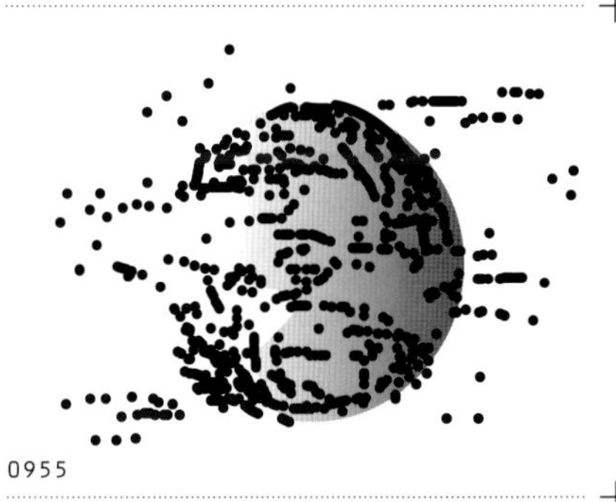

0955

0956

0957

0958

0959

0960

0961

0962

0963

0964

0965

0966

0967

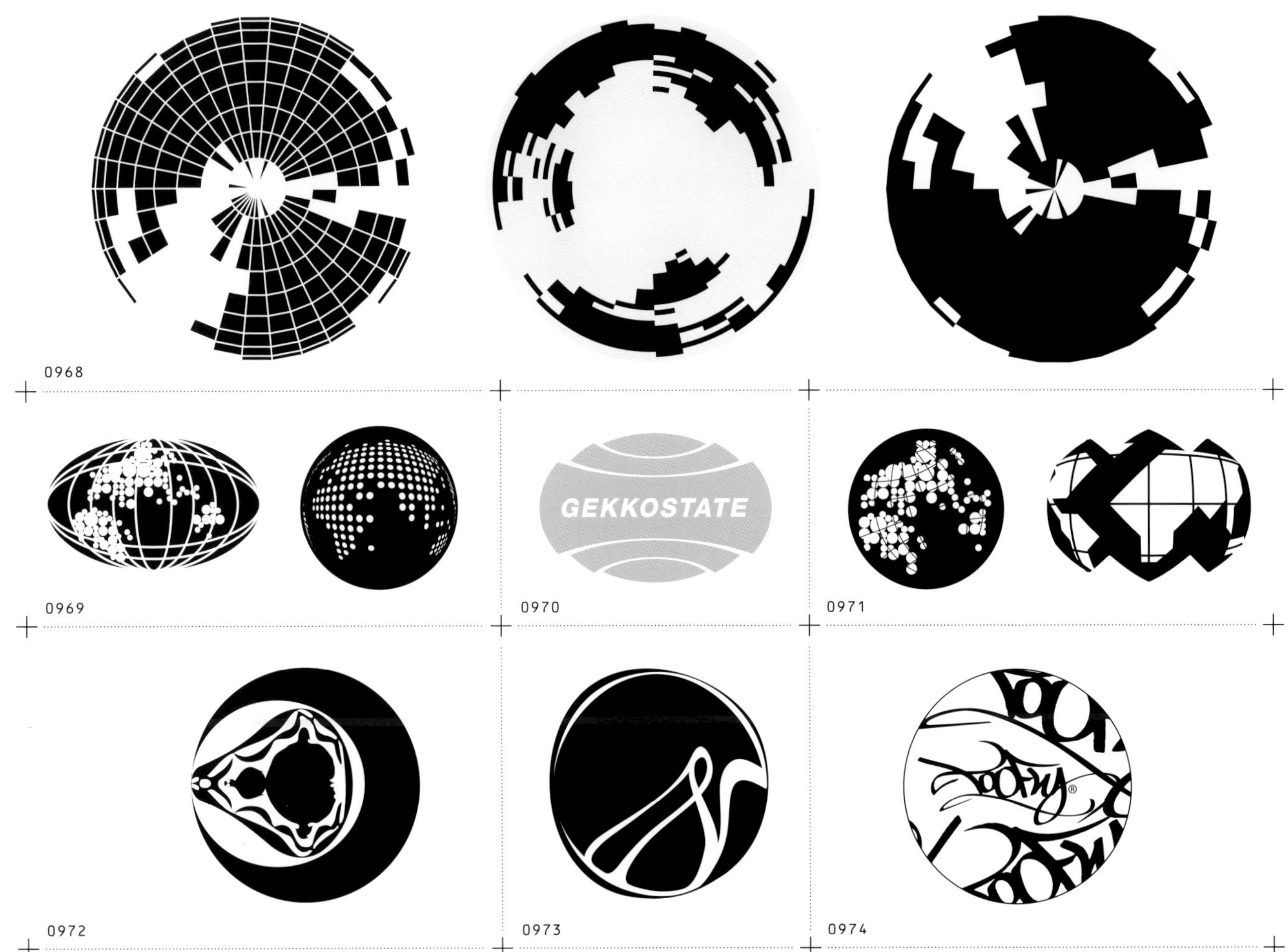

0968

0969

0970

0971

0972

0973

0974

0975

0976

0977

0978

0979

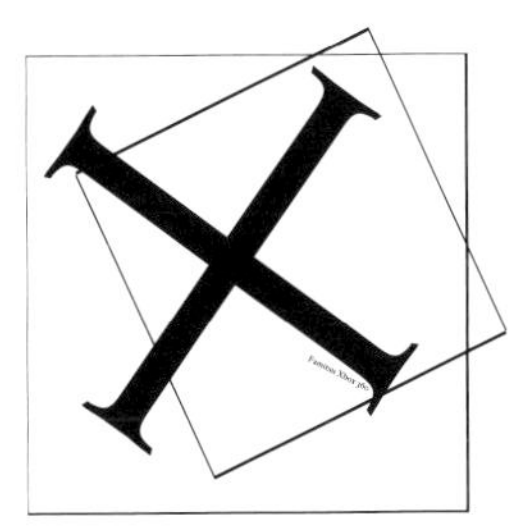

0980

0981

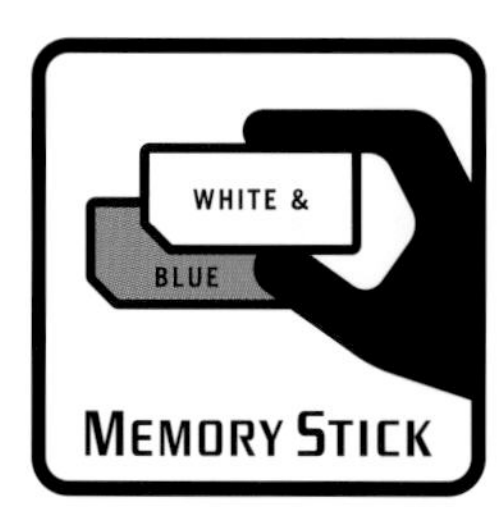

0982

0983

0984

0985

0986

0987

0988

0989

0990

0991

0992

GROUND TOUR

0993

0994

0995

最軟
最強

0997

0996

0998

0999

1000

1001

1002

1003

1004

1005

1006

1007

1008

1009

1010

1011

1012

1013

1014

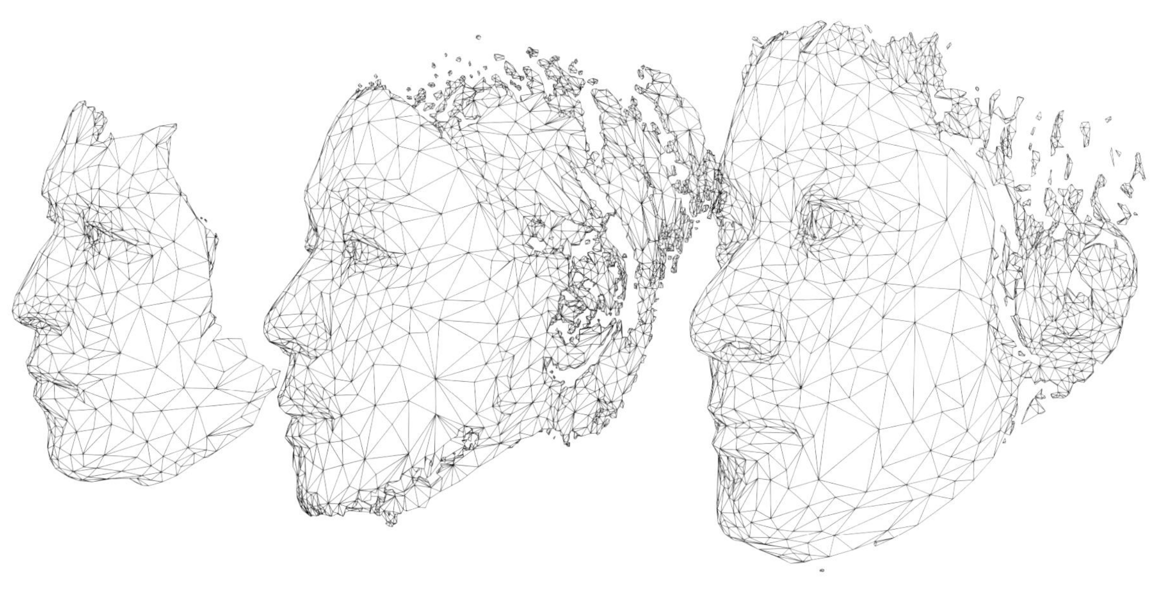

1015

1016

1017

1018

1019

1020

1021

1022

CHAOTIC
expression.
CONVULSIVE
POTENTIAL.
EQUAL RIGHT
FOR CYBONE
N6MAA10817
H.C. is music
which it is continuing
fighting in order
to carry out evolution
development.
POSITRON
ELECTRON
DEMAND
N6MAA10817
bass and guitar
noise, effected
and transformed
vocal sound,
and full of
"unexpected"!
N6MAA
10817

1024

1025

1026

1027

1028

1029

1030

1031

DFYFR
DON'T
FORGET
YOUR FIRST
RESOLUTION.

1032

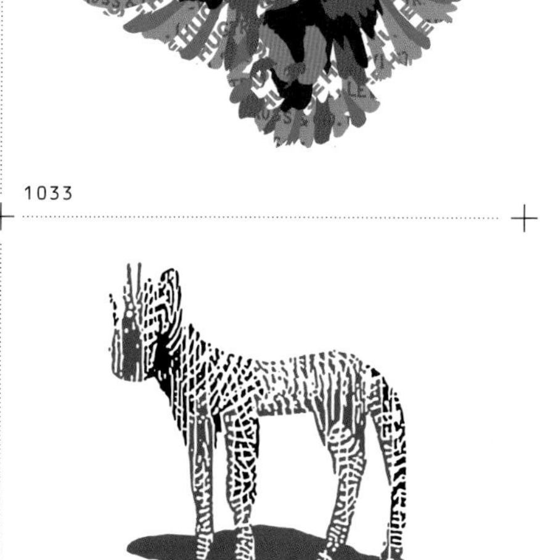

1033

1034

1035

1036

123™
KLAN
MESS WITH THE BEST
DIE LIKE THE REST
ORIGINAL GRAFFITI GANG SINCE 1992 ©

1037

1038

1039

1040

1041

1042

1043

1044

1045

1046

1047

1048

1049

1050

1051

1052

1053

1054

1055

1056

1057

1058

1059

1060

1061

1062

1063

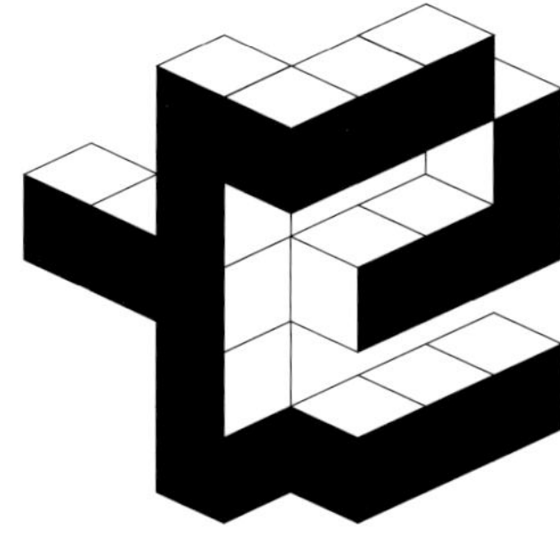
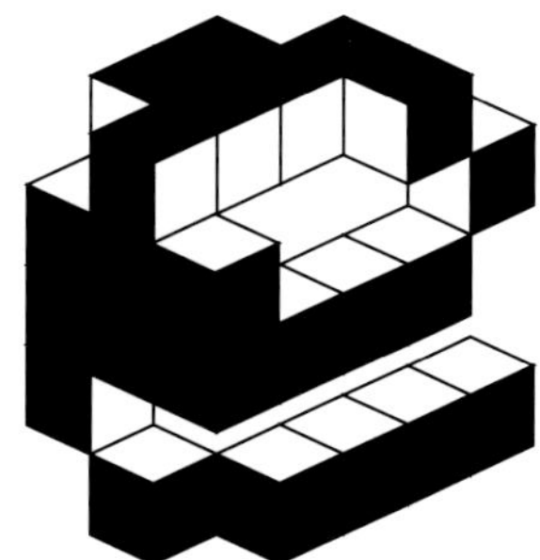
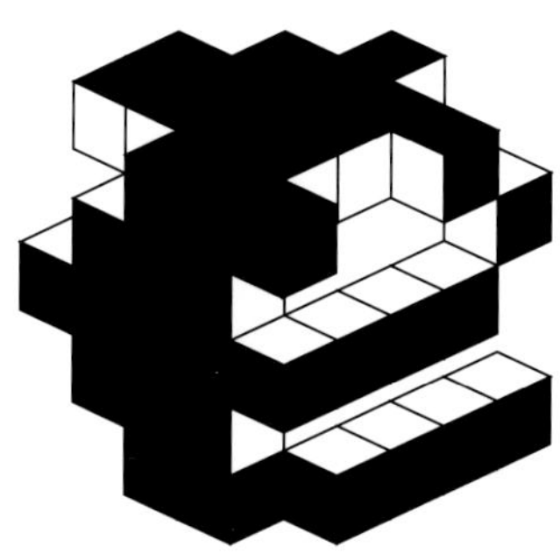

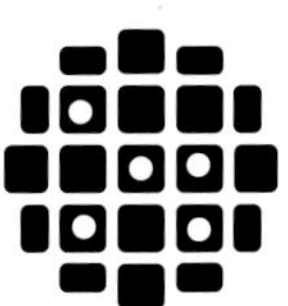

1064

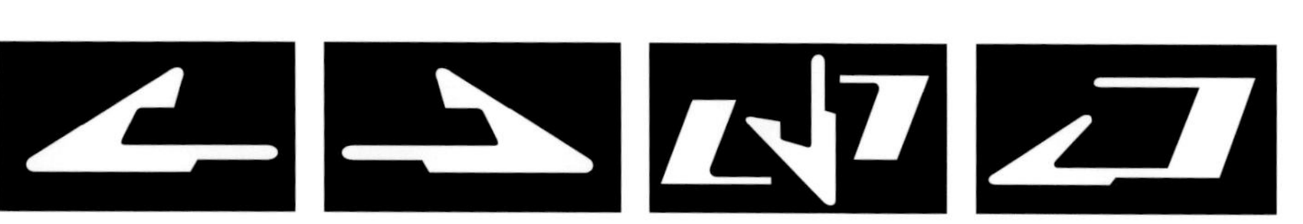

1065

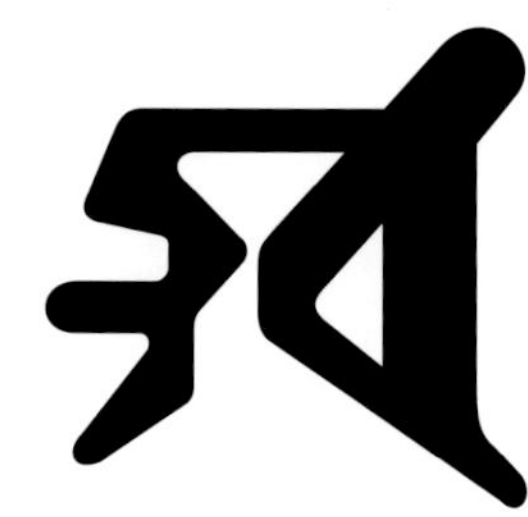

1066

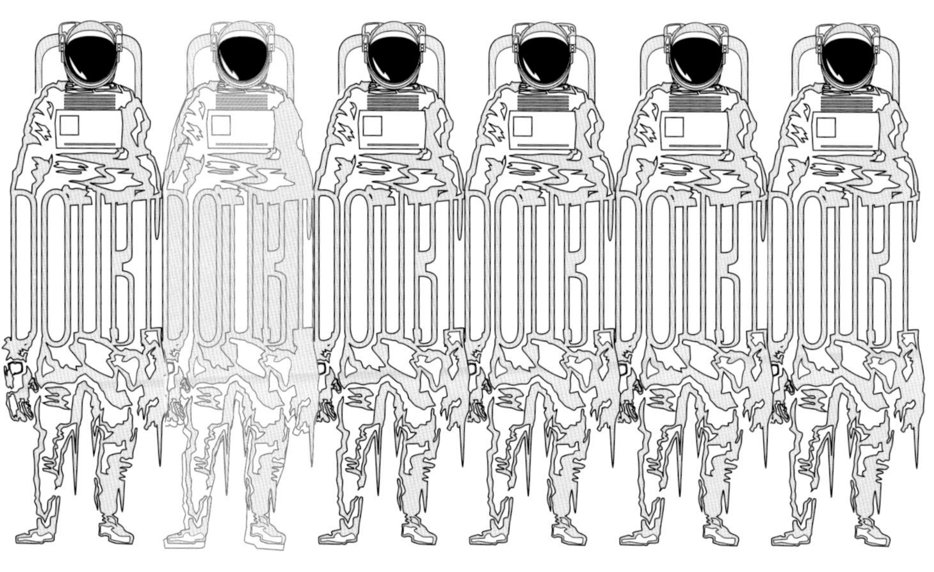

1067

1068

1069

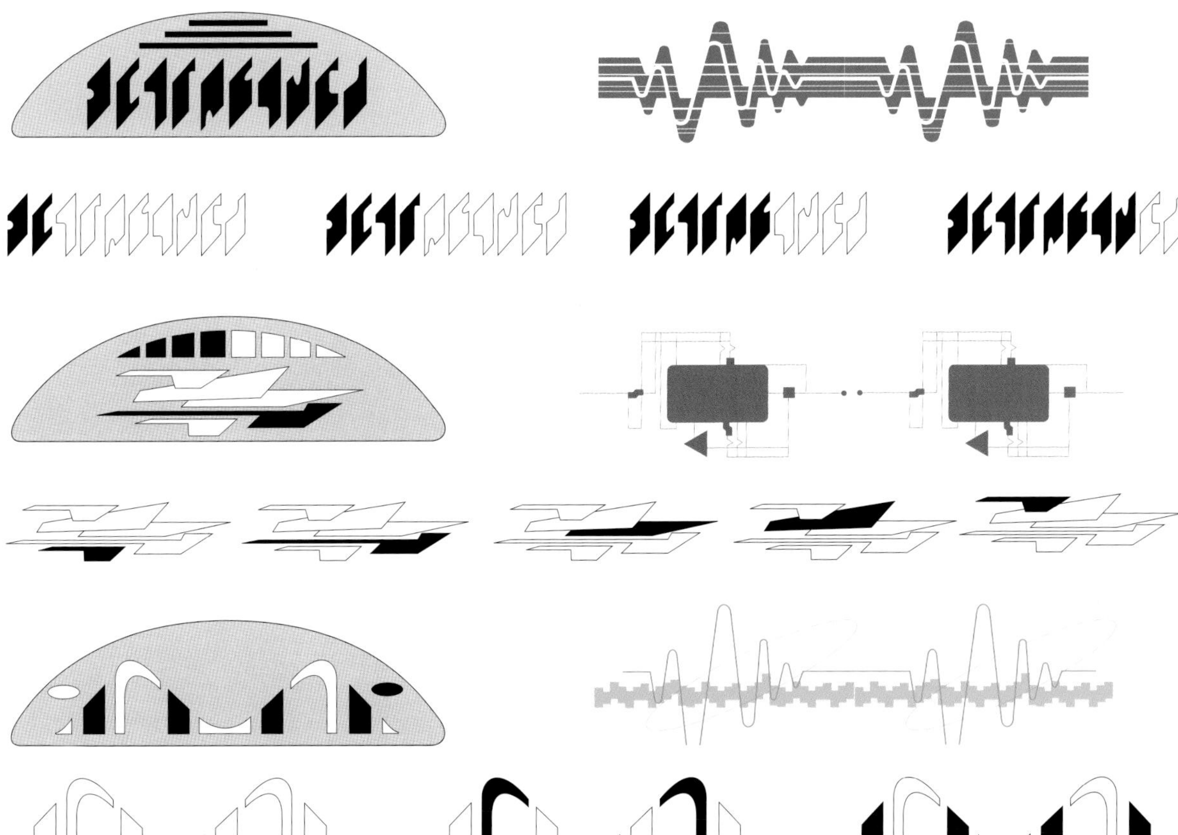

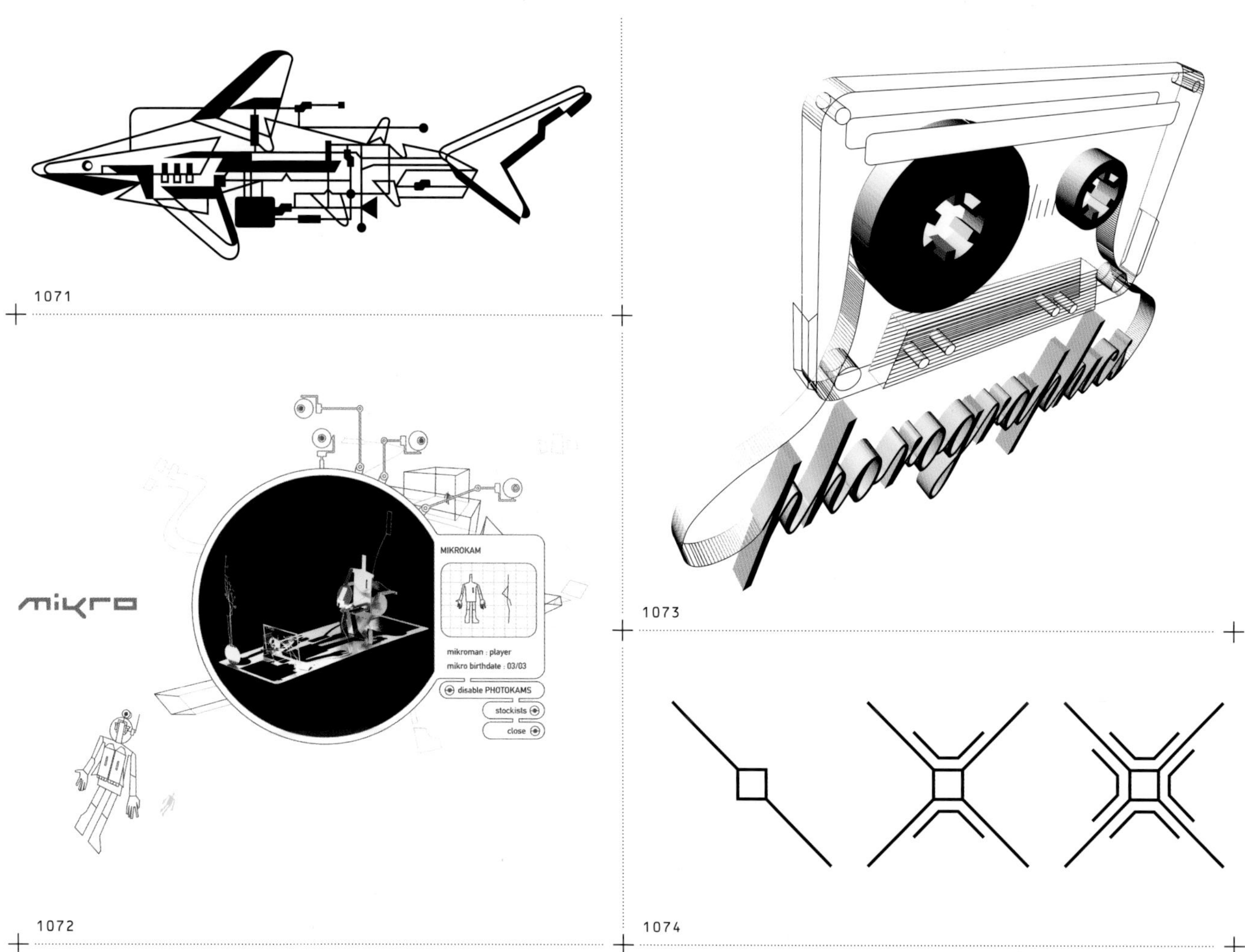

1071

1072

1073

1074

illustration

1075

1076

1077

1078

1079

1081

1082

1080

1083

1084

1085

1086

1087

1088

1089

1090

1091

1092

1093

1094

1095

1096

1097

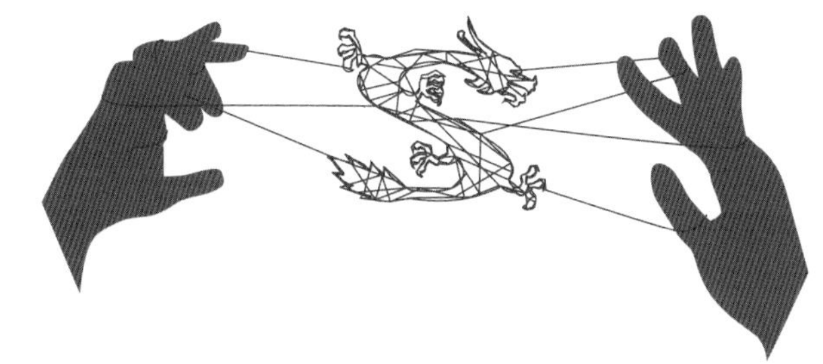

1098

1099

1100

1101

1102

1103

1104

1105

1106

1107

1108

1109

1110

1111

1112

1113

1114

1115

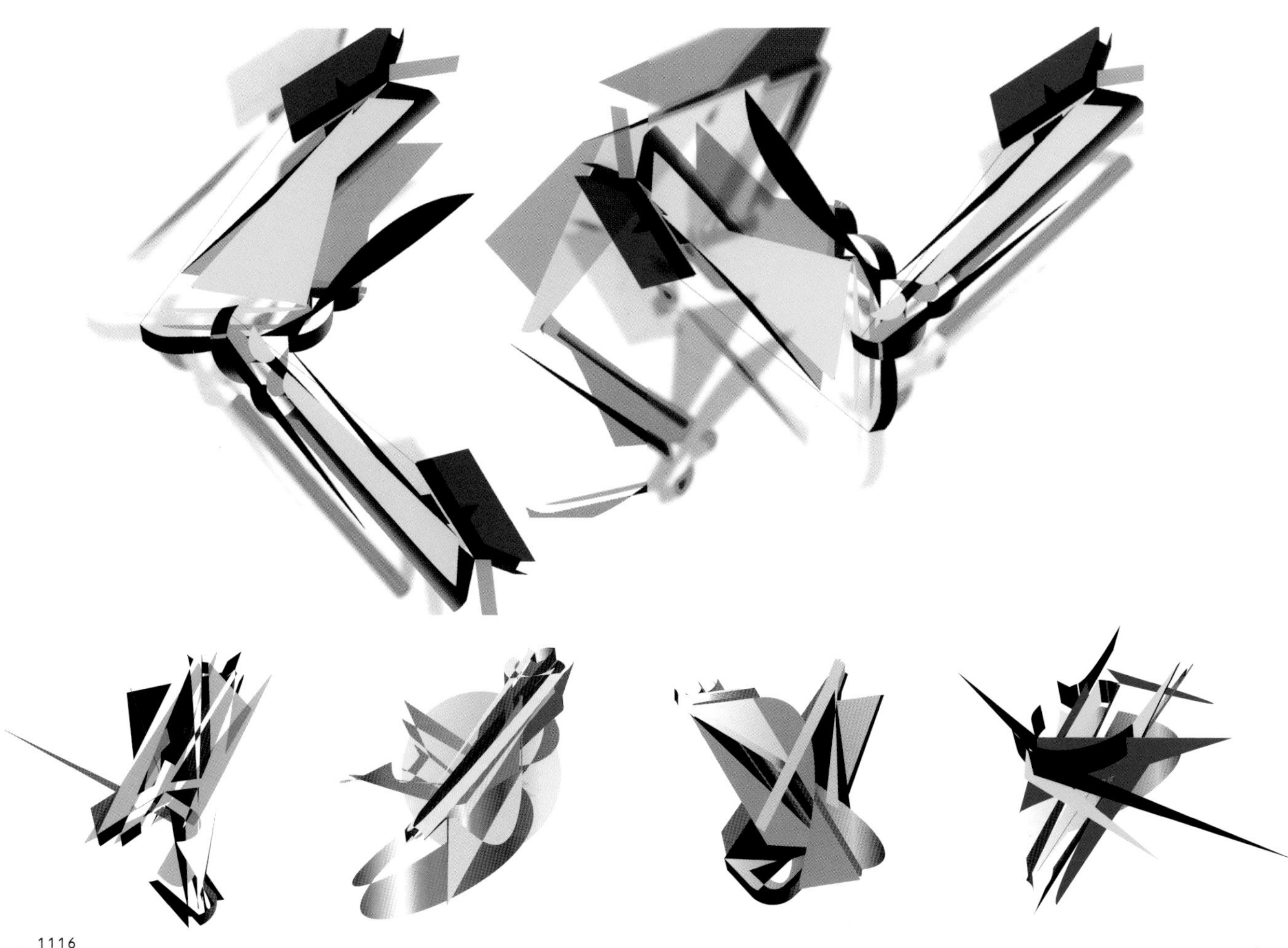

1116

1117

1118

1119

1122

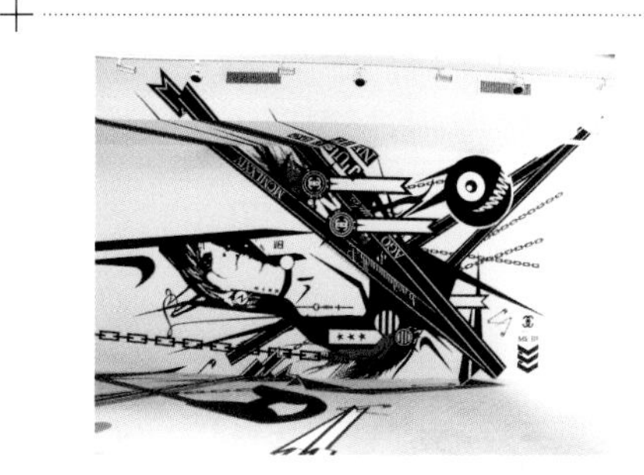

1120

1121

1123

1124

1125

1126

1127

1128

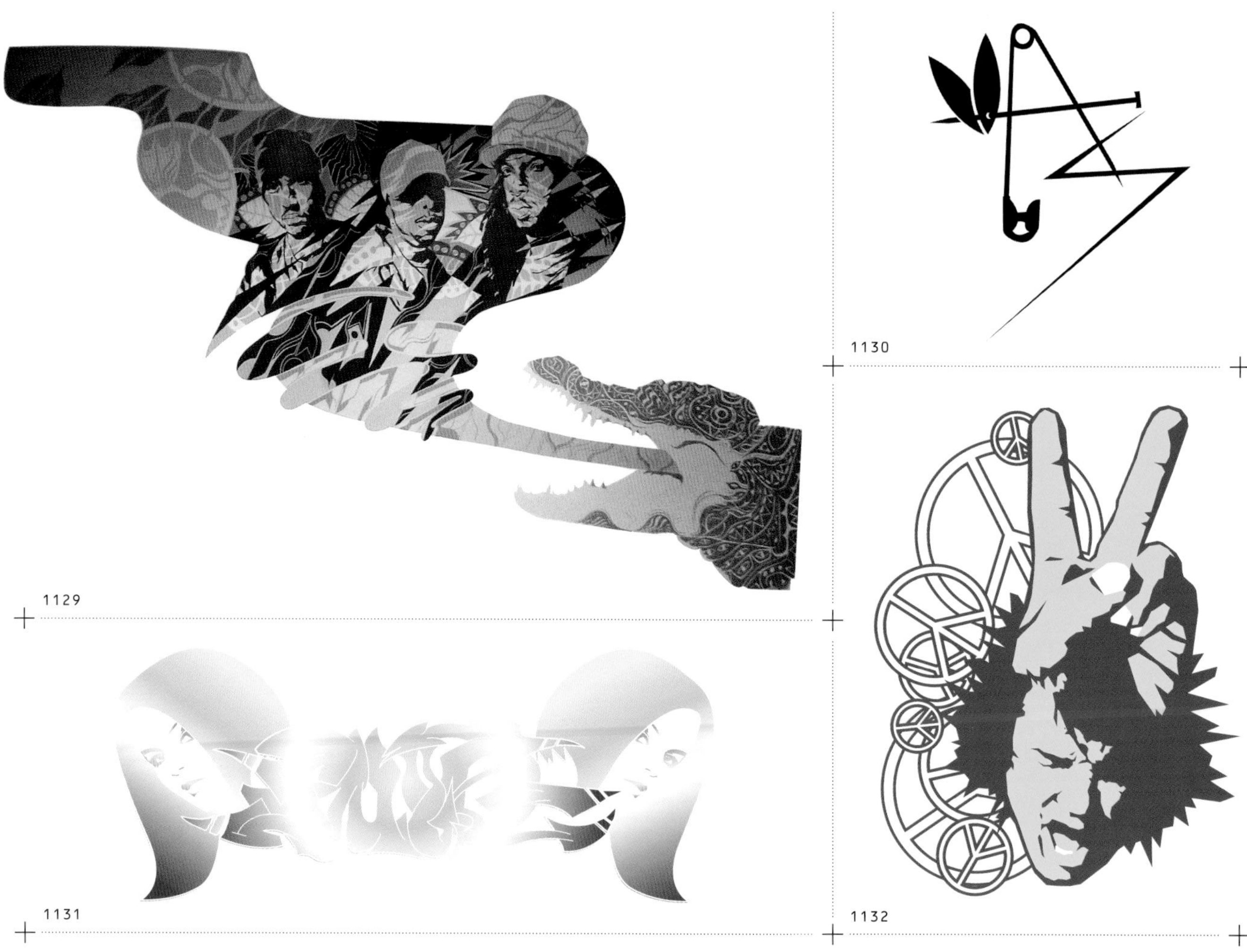

1129

1130

1131

1132

1133

1134

1135

1136

1137

1138

1139

1140

1141

1142

1143

1144

YUKI KOI

UN BEL DI VEDREMO
LEVARSI UN FIL DI FUMO

CHICAGO
YUKI KOI

1145

1146

1147

1148

1149

1150

DOLBY® keeps you ahead

1151

1152

1153

BEAT FROM THE BASEMENT VOLUME ONE
THE EMBROOKS
THE YOUNG PENNS
THE PEBBLES
LOS FEVERS
SIDE 1
THE EMBROOKS 'NO NO NO NO NO'
THE YOUNG PENNS
'THE MAN YOU'LL BE LOOKING FOR'
SIDE 2
THE PEBBLES 'EIGHT TO THE MAGIC'
LOS FEVERS 'YO GRITO'

1154

mid-late 60's Great Archives
ELECTRIC CIRCUS
SATURDAY
12th-FEB
at UFO CLUB
2000 OPEN 22:00
ADV·1300YEN (+DRINK 500YEN)
DOOR·2000YEN (W/1DRINK)
FREAKBEAT·PSYCHEDELIC·US GARAGE
SOFTROCK·TRANSWORLD·SIKEPOP·MOD
ACID FOLK & MORE!
LIVE ACT
DJ: EMILY·OKADA·SATOH·TANABE
TOKA... GUEST: YOSHIDA
PHYCHOTIC REACTION·
YOUNG PENNSYLVANIANS
from KOBE

1155

1156

1157

1158

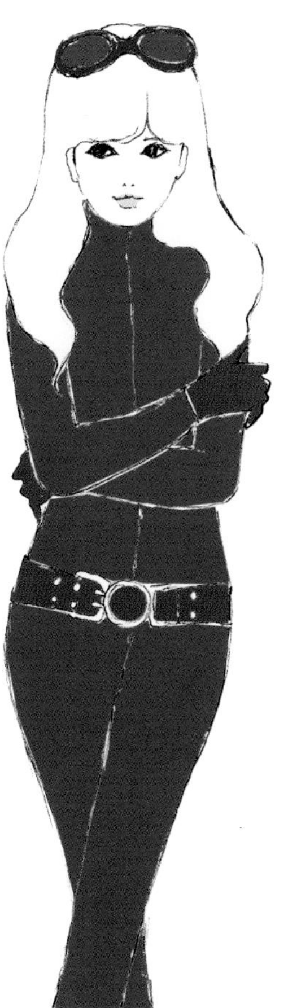

1159

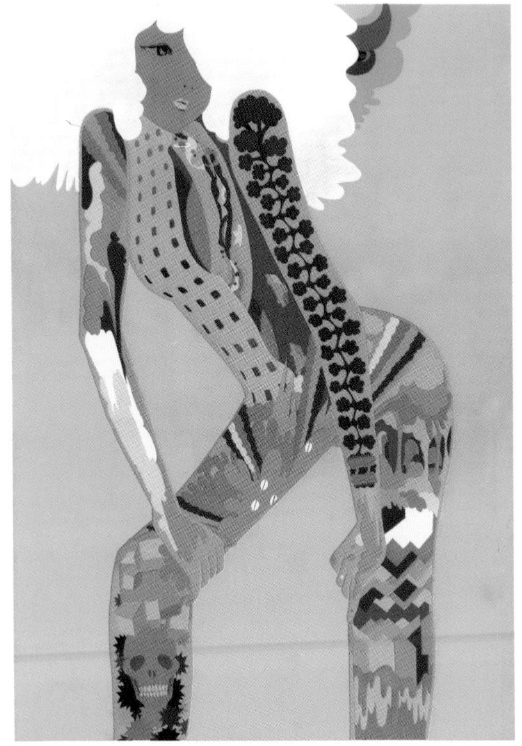

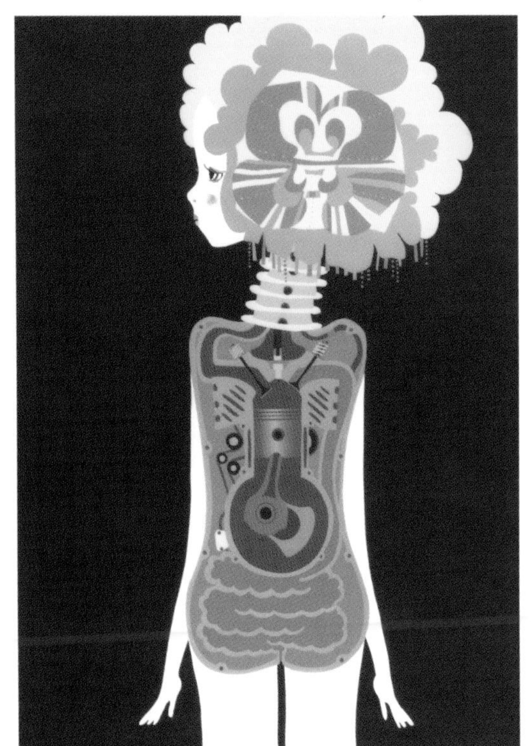

1160

1161

1162

1163

1164

1165

1166

1167

1168

1169

1170

1171

1172

1173

1174

1175

1176

1177

1178

1179

1180

1181

1182

ROBOSAPIENS

1183

1184

1185

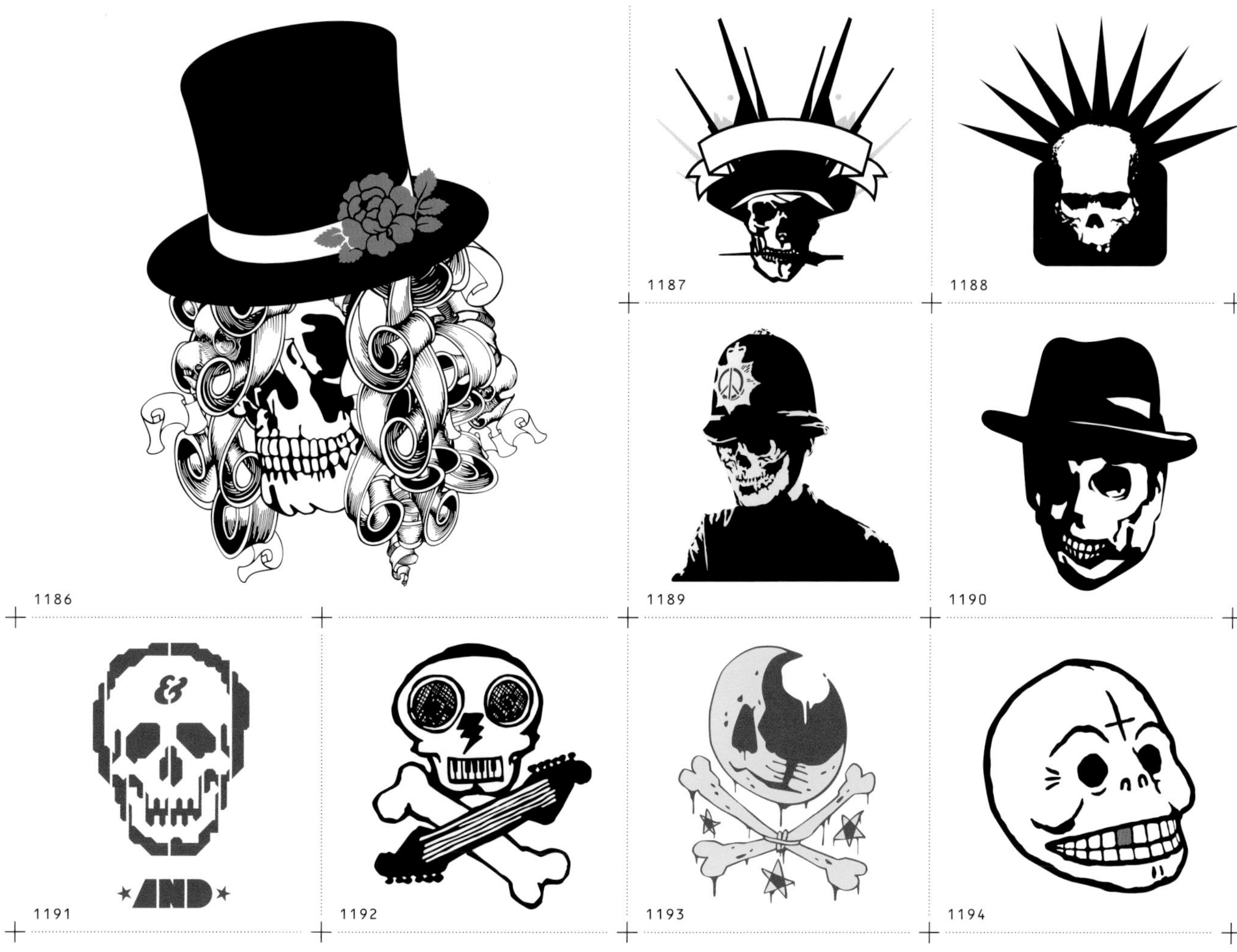

1186

1187

1188

1189

1190

1191

1192

1193

1194

1195

1196

1197

1198

1199

1200

1201

1202

1203

1204

1205

1206

1207

1208

1209

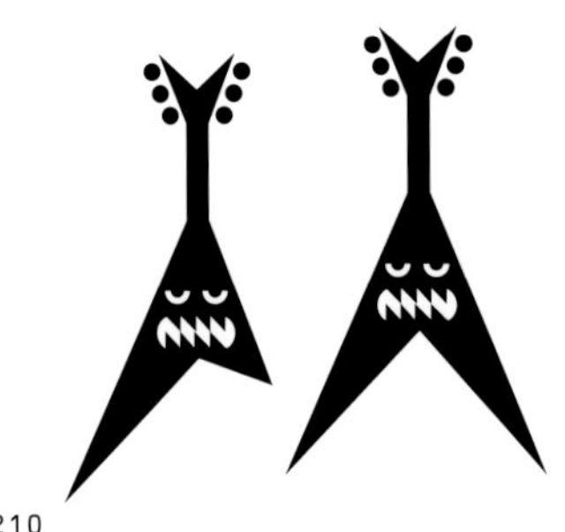

1210

1211

1212

1213

1214

1215

1216

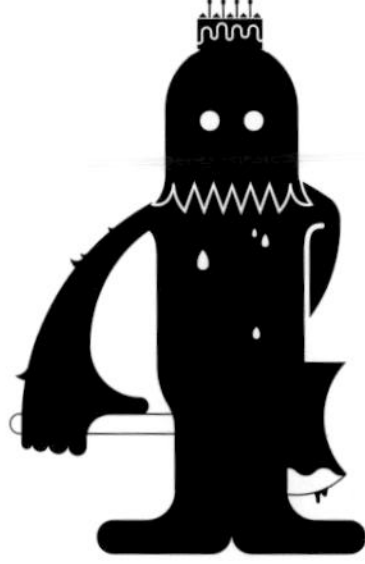

1217

fonts

ABCDEFGHIJKLMNOPQRSTUVWXYZ
abcdefghijklmnopqrstuvwxyz
,.0123456789!?#'=@=/+-"[]();:

1218

A B C D E F G H I J K L M N
O P Q R S T U V W X Y Z
0 1 2 3 4 5 6 7 8 9
! " # $ % & ' ( ) ~ = < > ? ÷ ± @

1219

1220

1221

あいうえお
かきくけこ
さしすせそ
たちつてと
なにぬねの
はひふへほ
まみむめも
やゆよゃゅょ

1222

アイウエオ
カキクケコ
サシスセソ
タチツテト
ナニヌネノ
ハヒフヘホ
マミムメモ
ヤユヨャュョ
ラリルレロ
ワヲンー
ァィゥェォ

1223

ABCDEFGHIJKLMNOPQRSTUVWXYZ
abcdefghijklmnopqrstuvwxyz
..0123456789'

1224

ABCDEFGHIJKLMNOPQRSTUVWXYZ
abcdefghijklmnopqrstuvwxyz,.0

1225

ABCDEFGHIJKLMNOPQRSTUVWXYZ
abcdefghijklmnopqrstuvwxyz

1226

1227

1228

ABCDEFGHIJKLMNOPQRSTUVWXYZ
abcdefghijklmnopqrstuvwxyz
,.0123456789!?'=@

1229

アイウエオ
カキクケコ
サシスセソ
タチツテト
ナニヌネノ
ハヒフヘホ
マミムメモ
ヤユヨ
ラリルレロ
ワヲン

1230

ABCDEF
GHIJKL
MNOPQR
STUVWX
YZ

1231

ABCDEF
GHIJKL
MNOPQR
STUVWX
YZ

1232

1233

1234

From modernism to indy: the history of typography

Hitoshi Nagasawa

It goes without saying that Macintosh changed the graphic design world from its very roots. The same holds true for typography production. Before Macintosh's popularization, typographical work involved a compass and straightedge, and typefaces that seemed almost like instruments of measure themselves were produced. If words are a means to express everything in the universe, then the graphic designer should, naturally, meticulously construct letters, which serve to retain records of words, as if measuring the world.

However, Macintosh changed all that. Adobe Illustrator's Bezier curve allows the graphic designer to bend and twist already existing fonts, while Photoshop allows the designer to mix colors with ease simply by overlapping and shifting askew layers of color. Macs allow designers to see what a completed design, like the layered palette of Knoll's famous corporate logo from the 1960s, will look like even before the design is actually taken to the printers.

A wide range of typography experiments took place in the United States at the Cranbrook Academy of Art in Michigan, as well as in West Coast surfing designs. The spirit of such experiments spread globally along with the personal computer, and the twentieth century faced a revolution in printing and typography of the same scale as that witnessed in Gutenberg's time.

This constitutes a huge transformation that includes technological changes owing to the personal computer. However, changes in twentieth-century art and graphic design connoted that such a transformation had taken place before then. For example, late nineteenth-century poet Stéhane Mallarmé's poem, *Un coup de dé jamais n'abolira le hazard* ("A Roll of the Dice will Never Abolish Chance"), appears visually composed so that large and small typeface sizes are organized into a design employing negative space. In the 1910s, Dadaists cut letters out of newspapers and magazines, destroying the normal conception of text being less than context. The Italian Futurist Fortunato Depero conceived of typographical architecture constructed of letters and even built a full-scale model.

These events and movements took place between the 1910s and early 1920s. Before the Bauhaus developed modern design, the avant-garde movement in Western Europe — including the Russian Constructivists — had already taken an interest in and heightened their awareness of typography.

The Birth of Modern Typography

What we recognize today as the most perfected typefaces are known collectively as "Swiss typography." Naturally, Helvetica and Univers are popular fonts included in personal computer software, and few graphic designers are unfamiliar with these names.

The Bauhaus took on and continued to experiment with the modernism of Swiss typography before World War II. The Bauhaus was founded in Weimar in 1919 and moved to Dessau in 1925 before the Nazis finally shut down the school. The trends of the day influenced the Bauhaus, and education at the school became the forerunner to all aspects of modernism in the twentieth century.

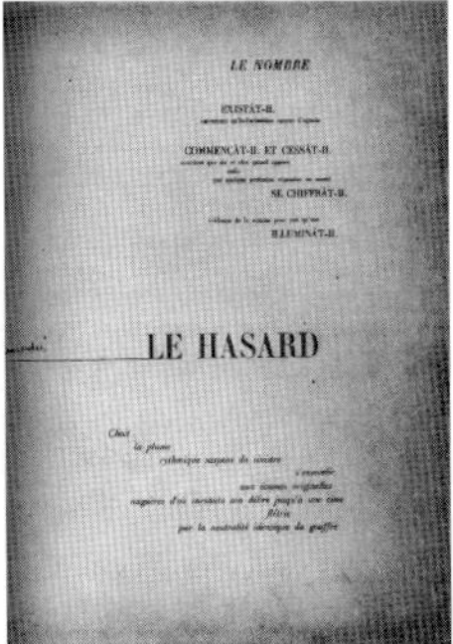

Stéhane Mallarmé's poem *Un coup de dés* ("A Roll of the Dice") was first published in1897. Mallarmé's poem is not relevant specifically to the development of typography, so much as it is revolutionary thanks to Mallarmé's use of large and small print, his use of margins and negative space, and his use of layout to match the poem's contents. For its day, this poem was also unparalleled in terms of content.

This work reflects the "Universal" font, a new design of lowercase typeface created by Bauhaus professor Herbert Bayer in 1928. Universal became the model for the Bauhaus, which favored lowercase.

One of the characteristics of the Bauhaus's modernism is the favoring of lowercase letters in typography. The use of both capital and lowercase letters engenders inequality. Lowercase letters in sans serif typeface (which means typeface "without serif," where "serif" refers to extensions of strokes on letters, rendering all strokes of equal thickness) are able to express everything using the minimum number of letter styles. It also reduces the sense of inequality created when capital and lowercase letters are combined and promotes efficiency in typing and phototypesetting. It is a style devised by an extremely functionalist mindset.

While the typeface adopted by the Bauhaus's Dessau school was not composed solely of lowercase letters, its geometric sensibility did symbolize the directions the school took in its typographical teachings. Incidentally, the 1920s German designer Paul Renner created Futura, a font commonly used today, which seems to contain Bauhaus influences.

Strictly speaking, all that modern typography is does not comprise the Bauhaus. As mentioned above, the avant-garde movement of the early twentieth century also served as a catalyst in its creation. However, the Bauhaus was responsible for giving direction to previously indistinct movements, dubbing them "modernism" and "internationalism." That is to say, the Bauhaus gave birth to the modern aesthetics, and in one sense it marked the inception of globalism that is leveling the world.

Then in 1928, talented designer Jan Tschichold schematized Western trends in Modernism in his book, *Die Neue Typographie* (*The New Typography*). This served as the textbook for modern typography thereafter.

Swiss Typography

As Nazism rose in Germany, talented artists were forced into exile or killed. Members of the Bauhaus fled to Switzerland, which maintained neutrality during World War II. Moreover, in the 1930s, in Germany and in the Soviet Union, the Nazis and Stalin began to take control over and standardize art and aesthetics, whether under the pretext of "nationalism" or "socialism." Meanwhile, in Switzerland modernists continued to thrive unmolested and develop modern design.

After the war, circumstances led to the blossoming of modern typography in Switzerland. For example, after the war Bauhaus member and designer Max Bill, who during the war was active in Switzerland, became the first director of *Hochschule für Gestaltung Ulm* ("The Ulm School of Design"), which continued the aims of the Bauhaus.

Such an environment allowed the birth of the now classic typeface Helvetica. Max Meidinger, who developed Helvetica, spent several years designing it for the typeface foundry Haas. He finally completed the exquisitely refined and elegant typeface in 1957. The typeface was originally dubbed *Neue Haas Grotesk* (Gothic typefaces are referred to as "grotesk" in Germany, while in France they are called "antique"). The Haas Foundry later sold the rights to the typeface to D. Stempel AG, who changed the name to Helvetica, which is the Latin for Switzerland.

The supposed intention behind Helvetica's creation was to have a typeface that would allow translations in all four of Switzerland's official languages to appear attractively on a single page.

Adrian Frutiger designed Univers, another common Swiss typography font, in 1957. Frutiger is also known for designing the sophisticated typeface Optima. Univers went on to become the most popular typeface in the Netherlands.

Once graphic design became possible using a personal computer, Helvetica and Univers were the first fonts available as software. In other words, these two typefaces have come to typify what should be considered classic modernism.

However, let us not forget Alexey Brodovitch, who was responsible for popularizing modernism in art direction and editorial design before modern typography became a definable entity in the 1950s. In the 1930s Brodovitch became the art director of the fashion magazine *Harper's Bazaar*. He used bold layouts that bleed into the margins, was meticulous in his selection of photographs, produced elegant typography designs, and made sophisticated use of serif and sans serif typefaces. Brodovitch's work may be considered legendary in all of these aspects.

While one would expect *Harper's* rival, *Vogue*, to act in opposition to Brodovitch's refined taste, *Vogue* instead revamped its own cover design, indicating that Brodovitch's achieved more than just the designs he produced himself.

The 1950s to 1960s were a period during which modernism became refined and notably popularized. Everyone believed in the "future" and "progress" and stopped looking back to past aesthetics. Art nouveau and art deco became completely forgotten, and anything that was "new" or "simple" was deemed beautiful.

Nostalgia and the Backlash against Functionalism

The international popularity of Swiss typography and modern design resulted in the abandonment of "past history" and "heritage," while making them symbols of functional aesthetics and capitalist wealth. However, as capitalism and functionalism became more advanced, youths rebelling against this "adult" world and commercialism began to appear.

Psychedelia colored youth culture in the latter half of the 1960s. The circumstances of the day gave birth to this movement. Said to have originated in 1964 with a hand-drawn poster for the West Coast band the Charlatans, urban culture and drug culture combined their influences to create the psychedelic movement. Later, almost all West Coast band posters became handmade.

Then in 1965 the University of California held the Jugendstil and Expressionism Exhibition. After viewing a poster created around 1910 by Viennese secessionist Alfred Roller at the exhibition, designer Wes Wilson produced a poster in April 1966 composed of undulating and rounded typography that would come to symbolize psychedelia.

The Fillmore, a club operated by Bill Graham, directly reflected the West Coast's new youth culture of this era, and many psychedelic poster artists made their names creating posters for live performances at the Fillmore. There were at least thirty famous poster artists associated with the Fillmore, including Victor Moscoso, Bonnie MacLean, and Stanley "Mouse" Miller. These artists reached a pinnacle during the Summer of Love in 1967, which witnessed the design of a grand array of typography.

It is believed that during the "psychedelic era," which lasted from 1966 to 1971, approximately 550 different posters were designed and about 200,000 were printed. While this does not mean that psychedelia invaded the commercial world, which represented the most mainstream culture, typography used in ads for haute couture magazines did at least display undulating, hand-rendered forms, illustrating the actual extent of the psychedelic movement during this time.

May '68 and Situationism

The era of the psychedelic revolution, which was rooted in youth-culture aesthetics and acid experimentation, was also the age of student power. The youth of the psychedelic era constituted the driving force behind the antiwar movement against involvement by the U.S. and European nations in the Vietnam War.

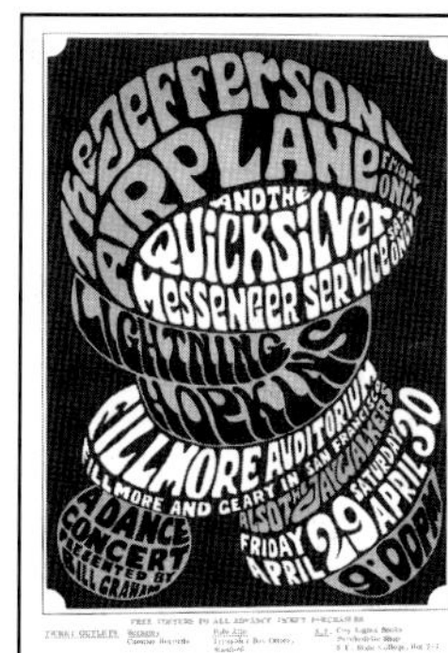

Wes Wilson designed this poster for a live performance at Fillmore in April 1966. Typography of psychedelic, undulating forms became established around this time.

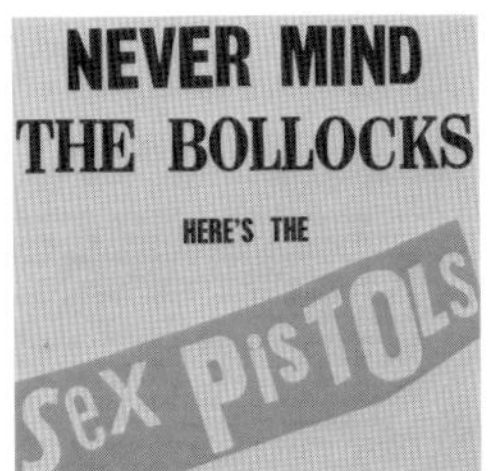

© Jamie Reid
Jamie Reid produced the design for the Sex Pistols first album cover.

Then in Paris the revolution that became known as "May '68" occurred. Laborers and others became wrapped up in what started as a student movement, and on May 21 a massive demonstration involving several million people broke out around France, primarily in Paris. President Charles De Gaulle's conservative administration collapsed the following year as a result.

Changes occurred in socialist nations around this time as well. In 1968 the Soviet Union intervened in Czechoslovakia to crush the "liberalization" promoted by the Dubcek regime, which became known as "Prague Spring." The same year saw the widespread strikes and demonstrations in France. However, thirty years later graphic design played a prominent role in the methods used by students in Yugoslavia opposing Milošević's dictatorship to collapse his regime (cf. works appearing under the Otpor movement for reference)[1].

Protestors referred to as "situationists" wrote political graffiti on street corners in Paris during May '68. Malcolm McLaren, known for later producing the punk rock group the Sex Pistols, was present in Paris and interacted with the situationists. Jamie Reid, the artist responsible for the artwork on the Sex Pistols album covers, was also in France participating with McLaren. Reid later designed the historical album covers for *Never Mind the Bollocks* and *The Great Rock 'n' Roll Swindle*. Reid's style of typography may possibly be considered the largest departure from Swiss typography.

The distinguishing characteristics of the Sex Pistols and punk graphism lay in a typography consisting of reassembled letters that had originally been cut out of newspapers and magazines. This approached echoed that adopted by Dadaists in the 1910s.

Punk, a movement often associated with destruction and despair, perfectly resonated with the sensibilities of Dadaist design. McLaren and Reid, who had witnessed May '68, carried home to England the spirit of this revolution and applied it to punk graphism, defining their generation. This act could be seen as more thoroughly antisocial when compared to the hippy generation, which displayed disillusionment but ultimately returned to society. This total rebelliousness may be the aspect that causes punk to still appeal to many young people, to cross generations, and to have given rise to the neo-punk movement.

New Wave and Neville Brody

Punk's heyday was short. Audiences grew bored with the monotonous three-chord songs. "Fashion punk" appeared as a commercialized version of punk fashion, allowing members of the mainstream to play tourist and sample the subculture's mode of dress. Punk became hollow. As with Dada, which evolved and became absorbed by surrealism, punk became absorbed by new wave.

The London designer Neville Brody appeared on the scene about the same time. Brody produced a variety of hand-drawn typography before computers were truly available for private use. The majority of Brody's designs consisted of independent record jackets and magazine layouts. His work during the 1980s was striking. He produced a large amount of fresh, innovative typefaces. Brody's Industria appeared in prominent advertisements and even became the first font software to be used on a Macintosh computer.

Brody's popularity was not limited to independent labels and London. The first collection of his works went on sale in 1988, and an exhibition of his work opened in Japan in 1990. In the same year, Brody collaborated with Jon Wozencroft to found the digital magazine *FUSE*. An array of graphic designers contributed to *FUSE*, which eventually published font software packaged on a CD-ROM. *FUSE* represented the vanguard in this respect, as well.

[1] "*Otpor!*" ("resistance!") was a movement organized in 1999 by university students demanding that former dictator Milošević democratize Yugoslavia. Many of these university students studied art, and the propaganda fliers and other literature distributed displayed astounding graphic design. One student devised *Otpor*'s logo of the fist, which later became recreated in CGI and developed into more intricate and advanced incarnations. *Otpor* was also responsible for creating its own humorous commercial films, such as one featuring Milošević being put into a washing machine and rinsed.

The most striking characteristic of design during the new wave era was that typography began to be produced and manipulated. Ian Swift, art director of London club and acid jazz magazine *Straight No Chaser*, used a stenciled style of typography, creating a new image for club jazz around 1990. Other graphic designers active in London were the group the Designers Republic and Paul White of Me Company fame. These designers were associated with house and other urban-culture-influenced musical trends.

In the mainstream world, on the other hand, Fabien Baron was performing typography experiments, such as taking gigantic letters and overlaying them with print of a different size. The majority of Baron's work was done for the fashion industry, and his designs overflowed with style. Madonna's notorious collection of nude photographs illustrates his novel approach to typography.

Innovativeness of the United States' West Coast

Most innovations in typography in the 1980s and 1990s took place in London. However, a new trend was beginning on the West Coast of the United States. Rudy VanderLans founded the magazine *Emigre* in 1984, the same year that Macintosh began sales of its first generation of personal computers. *Emigre* has enjoyed a long run and is still in publication today. From the start, Rudy VanderLans and his cofounder looked to the future of digital font.

In the early days there were difficulties in the computers' performances. However, Emigre font, which filled the large-format pages of *Emigre* magazine, was for a time indispensable to achieving a vanguard look in graphic designs. Then in the 1990s, once graphic design became truly possible using a Macintosh computer, Emigre font became the favorite of cutting-edge West Coast graphic designers. The graphics adopted by the skate culture of the time contained both conventional thrasher elements as well as experimental Emigre-style elements.

In the 1990s, while skateboarding and surfing aesthetics were combining with hip-hop graffiti to create multilayered aesthetics, Emigre came to play a central role in American design. David Carson, who was a former professional surfer and a high school social science teacher, served as the art director for the magazine *Ray Gun* from its inception. He produced exceptional, cutting-edge graphics. He would crop letters, use multilayered print, have letters touch, and manipulate the layout to the extent that the text would be rendered illegible. The aesthetics of the digital design age resided in his graphic designs.

In 1994 *Ray Gun* published a Brian Ferry interview using a font comprised entirely of symbols, rendering the interview illegible. The scandal still remains an unforgettable event in street design history.

David Carson's excessively experimental nature caused him to be replaced as art director. His work during his short engagement with *Ray Gun* was compiled into a single volume and published in 1995 under the title *The End of Print*. In 1997, a collection of his *Ray Gun* layouts were published in a book entitled *Ray Gun: Out of Control*. His use of carelessly cropped letters, lines littering the layout, layering of photographs to yield abstract images, and other experiments illustrate how much of a pioneer Carson was in 1990s graphic design.

Cranbrook Academy of Art

The Cranbrook Academy of Art in Michigan gave rise to new experiments in graphic design and typography in the United States when renowned designer, architect, and filmmaker Charles Eames met his future wife and artist Ray Kaiser.

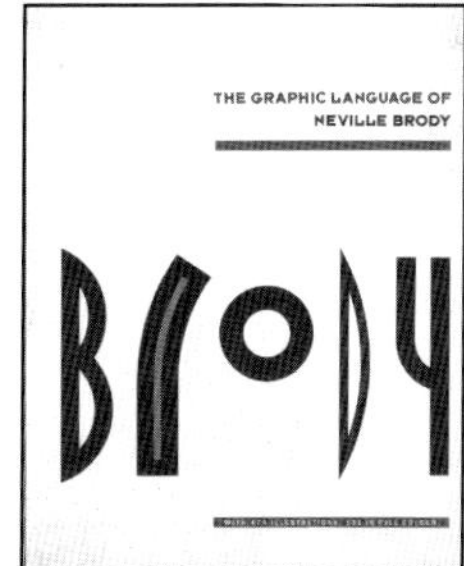

© 1988 Thames & Hudson Ltd. (Courtesy of Thames and Hudson Ltd.)
The Graphic Language of Neville Brody, published in 1988, was the first printed collection of Neville Brody's work. It later became a best seller and influenced graphic design in the 1990s. A second collection of Brody's works, *The Graphic Language of Neville Brody 2* was released for sale in 1994.

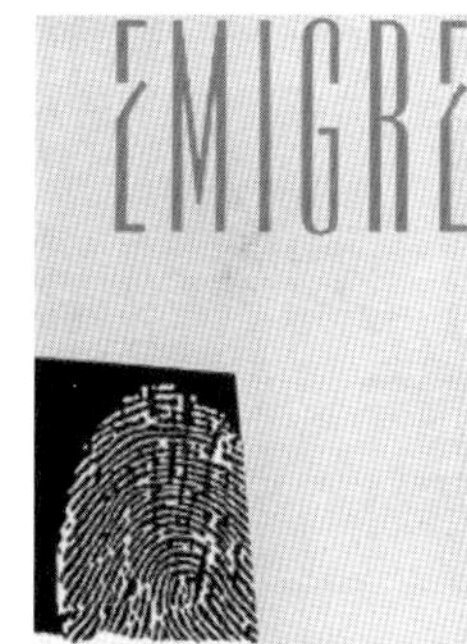

© Emigre, Inc.
Emigre was a cutting-edge magazine responsible for heightening recognition of typography in the 1980s.

At the time, graphic design using computers was liberating graphic designers from phototypesetting, block-copy making, and other processes that required a craftsman's skill, giving rise toward a predilection for cleaner, crisper designs. Moreover, three-dimensional graphics first appeared and became popular. Graphic designers using computers found conditions available to them in a single stroke, not unlike being in an ultra clean room free of contamination. In other words, graphic designers no longer had to worry about excess glue smudges or errant cuts and scratches from their craft knives, and when creating three-dimensional graphics, the designers merely dedicated themselves fully to smooth renditions. The loud, unintelligible aesthetics of Dada and punk were eliminated, and all aspects of the design became contained neatly within controlled parameters.

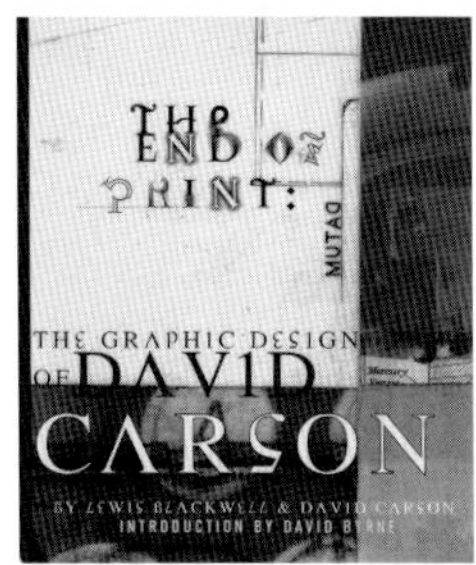

© 1995 Laurence King Publishing Ltd.
(Courtesy of Laurence King Publishing Ltd.)
David Carson's work of 1995, *The End of Print* is a cutting-edge collection of experiments in typography.

At this point in time, repeated experimentation using a computer to create loud designs, crop letters, or overlap text, creating layers took place at Cranbrook Academy of Art.

Katherine and Michael McCoy were teaching such design concepts around this time. The husband and wife team incorporated structuralism and new French philosophical ideas into their designs. Deconstruction (a popular movement encompassing philosophy and architecture) came into vogue, and the McCoy's experimented with it by adding lines that were irrelevant to the context and cutting letters into pieces.

It would be no exaggeration to say that graphic designs making extensive use of Photoshop's layer and blur functions originated with Cranbrook's students, who hailed from all over the world, and spread internationally from there.

Starting in the mid 1990s, Amsterdam, along with London and Antwerp, Belgium, came to symbolize the forefront of graphic design. This was owing largely to Robert Nakata, a graduate from Cranbrook Academy of Art and his codesigners.

In any event, the effects of the Cranbrook Academy of Art on graphic design history and, in particular, the introduction of Macintosh-aided design, is immeasurable. The same holds true for the achievements of Katherine and Michael McCoy. If graphic design history as taught in the academies established advertising design as the standard for graphic design without referencing these experiments, it would cause a tremendous problem in the contemporary graphic design field.

Moving Away from Graffiti, Layers, and Flatism

Hip-hop graffiti drawn in the New York subways and all over the Bronx accompanied the graffiti art rage that took place in the contemporary art of the 1980s. This constituted a total departure from the graphic design taught in the academies and was thus revolutionary, because it had developed free of any academic groundwork in graphic design.

Not only did hip-hop music, which was born on the streets and featured two turntables and a mixer, give rise to breakdancing, but also its graffiti engendered a form of graphic design.

Graffiti in the 1990s became, in a certain sense, more formalized than that of the 1980s. After 2000 a new, adaptable form of graffiti began to emerge from the musical fusion of hip-hop, electronica, and other new experiments.

As graffiti artwork similar to or even more interesting than contemporary art appeared, graphic designers began to create fonts mimicking graffiti in the software arena. As expected, the ties between urban music and graphic design culture cannot be dissolved, and should be linked together forever.

In that respect, computer-assisted graphic design in the 1990s was directly linked to techno music. Starting in 1989, techo music took Europe and the rest of the world by storm. It also impacted graphic design from various fronts, and its influence on typography was significant. Numerous graphic designers began to produce techno-influenced typography. Not limited to Europe, graphic designers in Japan and Hong Kong could also be observed following this trend.

It was within this context that the British design company Tomato was founded. Tomato broke new ground using Photoshop's layer tools. The band Underworld, part of the company, serves to link its designs and dance music.

However, flatism and nondesign emerged in the late 1990s as a reaction against graphic designs brimming with multilayered experimentation as produced by David Carson, Tomato, and other designers.

This is linked to the concept of light architecture and "superflat" in the fields of architecture and the fine arts, respectively. Swiss typography became swiftly reinstated during this time. Graphic designers previously unfamiliar with Swiss typography could be heard declaring minimalism and Swiss type as their favorite styles. Magazine layouts became extremely uniform as a result. Article titles would appear in plain, crisp, smallish Helvetica typeface. Everyone sought a homogeneous, clean crispness and thought that constituted stylish.

However, fads don't last very long.

Past retro designs rooted in the 1960s (in illustration, typography, and other fields) have moved toward 1970s retro, which is now enjoying a sudden resurgence. The public and designers have been tiring of minimalism. Tastes reflected in the experimentations of innovative designers have been shifting toward neo-baroque since 2003, transforming it into today's great vogue.

If the personal computers are responsible for spreading personalized graphic design and typography on a global scale, the Internet has made up for a lack of a distribution framework.

Graphic designs are distributed on a grand scale through advertisements and major magazines. However, a computer and the Internet enable design groups incapable of mass distribution to inhabit the same world as the big players.

Computers will ensure the distribution of indy graphics in the twenty-first century.

Lastly, I would like to comment that as we put together this book, we relied heavily on the Internet to assemble the typography, icons, illustrations, and graffiti, primarily from Japan, but also from the rest of the world. Our world of graphic design, which seemed destined to be buried, began to be rescued from obscurity ever since the first Web browser, Mosaic, was developed at the National Center for Supercomputing Applications (NCSA) at the University of Illinois in 1993. We owe this to digital technology, and we fervently hope that this does not change in the future.

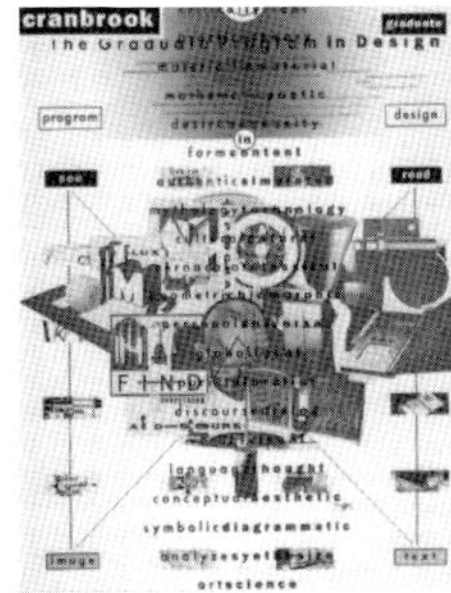

This is a piece a student attending Cranbrook Academy of Art produced in the early 1990s. The multilayered structure, borders, and letter positioning in this work, created using PhotoShop, are replete with novel experimentation.

index

0247 POSITRON
0248 Fujita Jiro Design
0249 papier colle
0250 Koji Takeuchi Graphic Design
0251 3deluxe
0252 POSITRON
0253 3deluxe
0254 POSITRON
0255 papier colle
0256 Taichi Ito [TARNICA]
0257 Planet Pixel Cologne
0258 ASYL CRACK
0259 POSITRON
0260 Jiro Takagi [Haus Graphic]
0261 EXTRACT
0262 papier colle
0263 Koji Takeuchi Graphic Design
0264 POSITRON
0265 POSITRON
0266 3deluxe
0267 Tsuyoshi Hirooka
0268 Zion Graphics
0269 Tsuyoshi Hirooka
0270 Jun Watanabe
0271 Colin Metcalf and Kevin Grady [GUM]
0272 Jun Watanabe
0273 papier colle
0274 Jun Watanabe
0275 PROTOTYPE DESIGNS
0276 milmake
0277 PROTOTYPE DESIGNS
0278 Masashi Ichifuru [TGB design.]
0279 POSITRON
0280 milmake
0281 milmake
0282 papier colle
0283 C100 Studio
0284 Shinji Shimada+Akiko Tauchi [vwv//design]
0285 Maniackers Design
0286 Munehiro Machida [NSSGRAPHICA]
0287 Maniackers Design
0288 Koji Takeuchi Graphic Design
0289 PROTOTYPE DESIGNS
0290 123KLAN
0291 Jiro Takagi [Haus Graphic]
0292 papier colle
0293 Hitoshi Nagasawa [papier colle]
0294 Koji Takeuchi Graphic Design
0295 Milkxhake
0296 Milkxhake
0297 Milkxhake
0298 POSITRON
0299 Koji Takeuchi Graphic Design
0300 Milkxhake
0301 nem [Shinji Nemoto]
0302 Milkxhake
0303 Hitoshi Nagasawa [papier colle]
0304 Milkxhake
0305 papier colle
0306 Jun Watanabe
0307 Jiro Takagi [Haus Graphic]
0308 Brandoctor
0309 Tsuyoshi Hirooka
0310 Tsuyoshi Hirooka ©manglobe
0311 Tsuyoshi Hirooka
0312 Maniackers Design
0313 papier colle
0314 Tsuyoshi Hirooka ©manglobe
0315 Tsuyoshi Hirooka
0316 Tsuyoshi Kusano ©2005 BONES / Project EUREKA・MBS
0317 papier colle
0318 Koji Takeuchi Graphic Design
0319 Megumu Kasuga [YiELD]
0320 Anonymous
0321 Tsuyoshi Hirooka
0322 Koji Takeuchi Graphic Design
0323 Megumu Kasuga [YiELD]
0324 papier colle
0325 papier colle
0326 EXTRACT
0327 Takeshi Hamada
0328 Shintaro Sakamoto
0329 Megumu Kasuga [YiELD]
0330 Koji Takeuchi Graphic Design
0331 A NEW PERSPECTIVE
0332 endoko [endo zuan koujyo]
0333 papier colle
0334 Tsuyoshi Hirooka
0335 Tsuyoshi Hirooka
0336 Takeshi Hamada
0337 Tsuyoshi Hirooka
0338 Maniackers Design
0339 Megumu Kasuga [YiELD]
0340 Anonymous
0341 Tsuyoshi Hirooka
0342 ZETUEI FONTS
0343 Jun Watanabe
0344 Tsuyoshi Hirooka ©manglobe
0345 Masashi Ichifuru [TGB design.]
0346 papier colle
0347 Shinji Shimada+Akiko Tauchi [vwv//design]
0348 Megumu Kasuga [YiELD]
0349 papier colle
0350 Masashi Ichifuru [TGB design.]
0351 Tsuyoshi Hirooka
0352 Megumu Kasuga [YiELD]
0353 Maniackers Design
0354 Tsuyoshi Hirooka
0355 ASYL CRACK
0356 Tsuyoshi Hirooka
0357 ZETUEI FONTS
0358 Koji Takeuchi Graphic Design
0359 Anonymous
0360 papier colle
0361 Tsuyoshi Hirooka
0362 Wataru Osakabe [Lovedesign co.]
0363 Tsuyoshi Hirooka
0364 Koji Takeuchi Graphic Design
0365 Tsuyoshi Hirooka
0366 Maniackers Design
0367 Tsuyoshi Hirooka
0368 ZETUEI FONTS
0369 Shinji Shimada+Akiko Tauchi [vwv//design]
0370 Takehiko Tsutsumi [ebc]
0371 Wataru Osakabe [Lovedesign co.]
0372 Tsuyoshi Hirooka
0373 Tsuyoshi Kusano
0374 papier colle
0375 Takehiko Tsutsumi [ebc]
0376 ZETUEI FONTS
0377 Dainippon Type Organaization
0378 SOUP DESIGN
0379 Tsuyoshi Hirooka
0380 Koji Takeuchi Graphic Design
0381 Megumu Kasuga [YiELD]
0382 Coa Graphics
0383 Maniackers Design
0384 Anonymous
0385 Anonymous
0386 Anonymous
0387 Anonymous
0388 EXTRACT
0389 Anonymous
0390 Anonymous
0391 Anonymous
0392 Anonymous
0393 Anonymous
0394 Anonymous
0395 Koji Takeuchi Graphic Design
0396 Megumu Kasuga [YiELD]
0397 ZETUEI FONTS
0398 Tsuyoshi Hirooka
0399 Wataru Osakabe [Lovedesign co.]
0400 Megumu Kasuga [YiELD]
0401 Takehiko Tsutsumi [ebc]
0402 Koji Takeuchi Graphic Design
0403 Wataru Osakabe [Lovedesign co.]
0404 Koji Takeuchi Graphic Design
0405 Dainippon Type Organaization
0406 Koji Takeuchi Graphic Design
0407 Koji Takeuchi Graphic Design
0408 Koji Takeuchi Graphic Design
0409 Koji Takeuchi Graphic Design
0410 Fujita Jiro Design
0411 Anonymous
0412 Koji Takeuchi Graphic Design
0413 Nobuo Yamada
0414 Anonymous
0415 Tsuyoshi Hirooka
0416 ASYL CRACK
0417 Takehiko Tsutsumi [ebc]
0418 Koji Takeuchi Graphic Design
0419 Tsuyoshi Hirooka
0420 Koji Takeuchi Graphic Design
0421 Anonymous
0422 Anonymous
0423 Koji Takeuchi Graphic Design
0424 Koji Takeuchi Graphic Design
0425 Koji Takeuchi Graphic Design
0426 Koji Takeuchi Graphic Design
0427 Koji Takeuchi Graphic Design
0428 BooLab.
0429 Tsuyoshi Hirooka
0430 Ayako Tsuboi [Sakurambo Kikaku]
0431 Dainippon Type Organaization
0432 ASYL CRACK
0433 Megumu Kasuga [YiELD]
0434 ZETUEI FONTS
0435 Hideaki Komiyama [TGB design.]
0436 Wataru Osakabe [Lovedesign co.]
0437 papier colle
0438 Tsuyoshi Hirooka
0439 Megumu Kasuga [YiELD]
0440 Megumu Kasuga [YiELD]
0441 papier colle
0442 Dainippon Type Organaization
0443 Dainippon Type Organaization
0444 Koji Takeuchi Graphic Design
0445 ZETUEI FONTS
0446 ZETUEI FONTS
0447 Dainippon Type Organaization
0448 Anonymous
0449 ZETUEI FONTS
0450 Jun Awano [Kaiteki]
0451 Tsuyoshi Hirooka
0452 Anonymous
0453 Megumu Kasuga [YiELD]
0454 Tsuyoshi Hirooka
0455 papier colle
0456 Dainippon Type Organaization
0457 SOUP DESIGN
0458 Megumu Kasuga [YiELD]
0459 Dainippon Type Organaization
0460 Ayako Tsuboi [Sakurambo Kikaku]
0461 Tsuyoshi Hirooka
0462 Tsuyoshi Kusano
0463 Takehiko Tsutsumi [ebc]
0464 coma [nadareshiki]
0465 BooLab.
0466 papier colle
0467 papier colle
0468 Tsuyoshi Hirooka
0469 Koji Takeuchi Graphic Design
0470 Koji Takeuchi Graphic Design
0471 Megumu Kasuga [YiELD]
0472 Koji Takeuchi Graphic Design
0473 Tsuyoshi Hirooka
0474 Anonymous
0475 Rinzen
0476 Hideaki Kato
0477 Tsuyoshi Hirooka
0478 White Noise
0479 papier colle
0480 Jakob Holmsberg
0481 Tsuyoshi Hirooka
0482 deep llp
0483 ASYL CRACK
0484 Tsuyoshi Hirooka
0485 deep llp
0486 Rogerio Lionzo
0487 Jakob Holmsberg
0488 weissraum.de(sign)
0489 Rogerio Lionzo
0490 Jakob Holmsberg
0491 Rinzen
0492 Koji Takeuchi Graphic Design
0493 milmake
0494 Wataru Osakabe [Lovedesign co.]

0495 weissraum.de(sign)
0496 weissraum.de(sign)
0497 Planet Pixel Cologne
0498 BooLab.
0499 Megumu Kasuga [YiELD]
0500 Hideaki Komiyama [TGB design.]
0501 Tsuyoshi Kusano
0502 Tsuyoshi Kusano
0503 Zucker & Pfeffer
0504 weissraum.de(sign)
0505 Gianni Rossi
0506 Jakob Holmsberg
0507 Rinzen
0508 Wataru Osakabe [Lovedesign co.]
0509 Jun Watanabe
0510 Masashi Ichifuru [TGB design.]
0511 WUFFDESIGN
0512 Tsuyoshi Kusano
0513 NOK Design
0514 TNOP_bePOSI+IVE design
0515 Urs Lehni
0516 Megumu Kasuga [YiELD]
0517 LOOT
0518 ASYL DESIGN
0519 Jun Watanabe
0520 SAFAUSTINA
0521 Koji Takeuchi Graphic Design
0522 UMBRUCH Gestaltung
0523 Tsuyoshi Hirooka
0524 3deluxe
0525 Tsuyoshi Hirooka
0526 LOOT
0527 3deluxe
0528 3deluxe
0529 LOOT
0530 Tsuyoshi Hirooka
0531 Zion Graphics
0532 Diverse Designer
0533 3deluxe
0534 3deluxe
0535 3deluxe
0536 3deluxe
0537 Tsuyoshi Hirooka
0538 POSITRON
0539 Diverse Designer
0540 LOOT
0541 LOOT
0542 LOOT
0543 LOOT
0544 LOOT
0545 LOOT
0546 LOOT
0547 LOOT
0548 LOOT
0549 Jun Watanabe
0550 LOOT
0551 LOOT
0552 ACT
0553 LOOT
0554 Yosuke Hamada
0555 LOOT
0556 Yosuke Hamada
0557 LOOT
0558 LOOT
0559 LOOT
0560 Yosuke Hamada
0561 ACT
0562 Yosuke Hamada
0563 LOOT
0564 LOOT
0565 LOOT
0566 Rick Falcon [Pro Wolf Master]
0567 ACT
0568 ACT
0569 LOOT
0570 LOOT
0571 3deluxe
0572 Zion Graphics
0573 Keita Soejima
0574 ALLRAID GRAPHICS
0575 LOOT
0576 ACT
0577 Tsuyoshi Hirooka
0578 Zion Graphics
0579 3deluxe
0580 Yoshiyuki Sano [HABIT DESIGN]
0581 Yoshiyuki Sano [HABIT DESIGN]
0582 Yoshiyuki Sano [HABIT DESIGN]
0583 Yoshiyuki Sano [HABIT DESIGN]
0584 Yoshiyuki Sano [HABIT DESIGN]
0585 Yoshiyuki Sano [HABIT DESIGN]
0586 Yoshiyuki Sano [HABIT DESIGN]
0587 Yoshiyuki Sano [HABIT DESIGN]
0588 Yoshiyuki Sano [HABIT DESIGN]
0589 Yoshiyuki Sano [HABIT DESIGN]
0590 Yoshiyuki Sano [HABIT DESIGN]
0591 Takeshi Hamada
0592 Fujita Jiro Design
0593 Yoshiyuki Sano [HABIT DESIGN]
0594 Yoshiyuki Sano [HABIT DESIGN]
0595 Coa Graphics
0596 Yoshiyuki Sano [HABIT DESIGN]
0597 Yoshiyuki Sano [HABIT DESIGN]
0598 LOOT
0599 Yoshiyuki Sano [HABIT DESIGN]
0600 Yutaka Tateyama
0601 Koji Takeuchi Graphic Design
0602 Zion Graphics
0603 red hot'n'cool
0604 3deluxe
0605 Jiro Takagi [Haus Graphic]
0606 papier colle
0607 papier colle
0608 papier colle
0609 papier colle
0610 papier colle
0611 papier colle
0612 papier colle
0613 Anonymous
0614 Takeshi Hamada
0615 Marc Atlan Design, Inc.
0616 Takeshi Hamada
0617 UENO★AMORE★HIROSUKE
0618 papier colle
0619 WUFFDESIGN
0620 ACT
0621 Mr. Invisible [Pro Wolf Master]
0622 VIER5
0623 Tsuyoshi Hirooka
0624 Diverse Designer
0625 Diverse Designer
0626 Dainippon Type Organaization
0627 Megumu Kasuga [YiELD]
0628 UMBRUCH Gestaltung
0629 papier colle
0630 Tsuyoshi Hirooka
0631 Tsuyoshi Hirooka
0632 Diverse Designer
0633 Mende Design
0634 Dainippon Type Organaization
0635 Zucker & Pfeffer
0636 VIER5
0637 Diverse Designer
0638 Megumu Kasuga [YiELD]
0639 Megumu Kasuga [YiELD]
0640 United States of the Art
0641 Eskim Dmitry
0642 United States of the Art
0643 papier colle
0644 papier colle
0645 Rosendahl Grafikdesign
0646 papier colle
0647 Megumu Kasuga [YiELD]
0648 POSITRON
0649 VIER5
0650 Tsuyoshi Hirooka
0651 Tsuyoshi Hirooka
0652 BooLab.
0653 Diverse Designer
0654 Masato Yamaguchi
[idea sketch international]
0655 SAFAUSTINA
0656 Tsuyoshi Kusano
0657 Tsuyoshi Kusano
0658 Tsuyoshi Hirooka
0659 Tsuyoshi Hirooka
0660 viagrafik
0661 Jun Watanabe
0662 3deluxe
0663 Jun Watanabe
0664 Jun Watanabe
0665 Masashi Ichifuru [TGB design.]
0666 Jun Watanabe
0667 viagrafik
0668 POWER GRAPHIXX
0669 viagrafik
0670 Shinji Shimada+Akiko Tauchi
[vwv//design]
0671 Megumu Kasuga [YiELD]
0672 Megumu Kasuga [YiELD]
0673 Megumu Kasuga [YiELD]
0674 ten_do_ten
0675 Rinzen
0676 Megumu Kasuga [YiELD]
0677 ten_do_ten
0678 ten_do_ten
0679 Megumu Kasuga [YiELD]
0680 Tsuyoshi Kusano
0681 sylvie lagarde+christophe lavergne
[restez vivants!]
0682 Takeshi Hamada
0683 sylvie lagarde+christophe lavergne
[restez vivants!]
0684 United States of the Art
0685 C100 Studio
0686 POSITRON
0687 Tsuyoshi Kusano
0688 Maniackers Design
0689 Jakob Holmsberg
0690 viagrafik
0691 Hatsumi Nonaka
0692 ZETUEI FONTS
0693 Masashi Ichifuru [TGB design.]
0694 papier colle
0695 3deluxe
0696 ZETUEI FONTS
0697 LOOT
0698 Megumu Kasuga [YiELD]
0699 Dopepope
0700 papier colle
0701 Hideaki Komiyama [TGB design.]
0702 SUPERDEUX
0703 papier colle
0704 papier colle
0705 Tsuyoshi Hirooka
0706 POWER GRAPHIXX
0707 Tsuyoshi Hirooka
0708 Melle/Dorland
0709 Melle/Dorland
0710 Marc Atlan Design, Inc.
0711 Dotzero
0712 enter98
0713 Amigos
0714 Designgruppe Koop
0715 RA GRADI
0716 Rosendahl Grafikdesign
0717 Seres Tamas
0718 WUFFDESIGN
0719 Zion Graphics
0720 PRESENT Design
0721 Takehiko Tsutsumi [ebc]
0722 Tsuyoshi Kusano
0723 Frank Rocholl
0724 Munehiro Machida [NSSGRAPHICA]
0725 Wataru Osakabe [Lovedesign co.]
0726 Lindedesign
0727 Hatsumi Nonaka
0728 ASYL CRACK
0729 Hideaki Kato
0730 Hideaki Kato
0731 LOOT
0732 ASYL CRACK
0733 Tsuyoshi Hirooka
0734 Tsuyoshi Hirooka
0735 Tsuyoshi Hirooka
0736 Tsuyoshi Hirooka
0737 Tsuyoshi Hirooka
0738 Tsuyoshi Hirooka
0739 Tsuyoshi Hirooka
0740 Tsuyoshi Hirooka
0741 Hideaki Kato
0742 Tsuyoshi Hirooka

0743 Tsuyoshi Hirooka
0744 ASYL CRACK
0745 Hideaki Kato
0746 Rinzen
0747 Nobuo Yamada
0748 Ai Fukasawa
0749 C100 Studio
0750 12ender GmbH
0751 3deluxe
0752 Tsuyoshi Hirooka
0753 Yutaka Tateyama
0754 Takeshi Hamada
0755 Takeshi Hamada
0756 Rinzen
0757 Red Herring Design
0758 papier colle
0759 papier colle
0760 Mende Design
0761 PING PONG DESIGN
0762 papier colle
0763 Tsuyoshi Hirooka
0764 papier colle
0765 Tsuyoshi Hirooka
0766 papier colle
0767 UK_DOUBT [Kentaro Ueno]
0768 papier colle
0769 UK_DOUBT [Kentaro Ueno]
0770 UK_DOUBT [Kentaro Ueno]
0771 Tsuyoshi Hirooka
0772 papier colle
0773 Glashaus Design
0774 papier colle
0775 LOOT
0776 Hintzegruppen
0777 papier colle
0778 C100 Studio
0779 yo-suke yamamoto
0780 POSITRON
0781 ZERO Headline Advertising
0782 Dotzero Design
0783 papier colle
0784 papier colle
0785 Heath Kane Design
0786 otpor
0787 otpor
0788 otpor
0789 otpor
0790 otpor
0791 otpor
0792 otpor
0793 otpor
0794 Hintzegruppen
0795 United States of the Art
0796 weissraum.de(sign)
0797 weissraum.de(sign)
0798 stilradar
0799 POSITRON
0800 POSITRON
0801 POSITRON
0802 POSITRON
0803 Hideaki Komiyama [TGB design.]
0804 POSITRON
0805 POSITRON
0806 POSITRON
0807 POSITRON
0808 papier colle
0809 papier colle
0810 papier colle
0811 Tsuyoshi Hirooka
0812 papier colle
0813 papier colle
0814 United States of the Art
0815 Var
0816 LOOT
0817 inTEAM Graphics
0818 Tsuyoshi Hirooka
0819 POSITRON
0820 papier colle
0821 Tsuyoshi Hirooka
0822 Tsuyoshi Hirooka
0823 Munehiro Machida [NSSGRAPHICA]
0824 POSITRON
0825 Tsuyoshi Hirooka
0826 POSITRON
0827 Tsuyoshi Hirooka
0828 papier colle
0829 papier colle
0830 papier colle
0831 Planet Pixel Cologne
0832 papier colle
0833 Dopepope
0834 papier colle
0835 papier colle
0836 papier colle
0837 papier colle
0838 Dopepope
0839 papier colle
0840 papier colle
0841 papier colle
0842 papier colle
0843 papier colle
0844 papier colle
0845 papier colle
0846 papier colle
0847 papier colle
0848 papier colle
0849 papier colle
0850 papier colle
0851 papier colle
0852 Rosendahl Grafikdesign
0853 Glashaus Design
0854 STRUKT
0855 papier colle
0856 papier colle
0857 papier colle
0858 LOOT
0859 papier colle
0860 Tsuyoshi Hirooka
0861 papier colle
0862 papier colle
0863 Tsuyoshi Hirooka
0864 ten_do_ten
0865 papier colle
0866 Planet Pixel Cologne
0867 Planet Pixel Cologne
0868 PenguinCube
0869 papier colle
0870 Tsuyoshi Hirooka
0871 Tsuyoshi Hirooka
0872 Tsuyoshi Kusano
0873 papier colle
0874 Tsuyoshi Hirooka
0875 Tsuyoshi Hirooka
0876 Tsuyoshi Hirooka
0877 Tsuyoshi Hirooka
0878 ten_do_ten
0879 Tsuyoshi Hirooka
0880 Tsuyoshi Hirooka
0881 Tsuyoshi Hirooka
0882 LOOT
0883 Tsuyoshi Hirooka
0884 Masashi Ichifuru [TGB design.]
0885 papier colle
0886 ten_do_ten
0887 Tsuyoshi Hirooka
0888 Tsuyoshi Hirooka
0889 papier colle
0890 ten_do_ten
0891 papier colle
0892 papier colle
0893 Tsuyoshi Hirooka
0894 Tsuyoshi Hirooka
0895 Tsuyoshi Hirooka
0896 POSITRON
0897 Tsuyoshi Kusano
0898 Tsuyoshi Hirooka
0899 Tsuyoshi Hirooka
0900 Tsuyoshi Hirooka
0901 papier colle
0902 UK_DOUBT [Kentaro Ueno]
0903 Tsuyoshi Hirooka
0904 Tsuyoshi Kusano
0905 Tsuyoshi Hirooka
0906 papier colle
0907 papier colle
0908 Planet Pixel Cologne
0909 papier colle
0910 ZETUEI FONTS
0811 Fujita Jiro Design
0912 sylvie lagarde+christophe lavergne
[restez vivants!]
0913 papier colle
0914 Tsuyoshi Hirooka
0915 TOOFLY [Maria Castillo]
0916 BooLab.
0917 substrat
0918 Shinji Shimada+Akiko Tauchi
[vwv//design]
0919 LOOT
0920 Fujita Jiro Design
0921 sylvie lagarde+christophe lavergne
[restez vivants!]
0922 Colin Metcalf and Kevin Grady [GUM]
0923 Tsuyoshi Hirooka
0924 Tsuyoshi Hirooka
0925 Fujita Jiro Design
0926 Tsuyoshi Kusano
0927 Tsuyoshi Kusano
0928 LOOT
0929 BooLab.
0930 Dopepope
0931 EXTRACT
0932 Tsuyoshi Hirooka
0933 Masashi Ichifuru [TGB design.]
0934 POSITRON
0935 Tsuyoshi Hirooka
0936 United States of the Art
0937 POSITRON
0938 Yoshiyuki Sano [HABIT DESIGN]
0939 TOOFLY [Maria Castillo]
0940 Tsuyoshi Kusano
©2005 BONES / Project EUREKA・MBS
0941 TOOFLY [Maria Castillo]
0942 Tsuyoshi Hirooka
0943 LOOT
0944 POSITRON
0945 papier colle
0946 POSITRON
0947 LOOT
0948 POSITRON
0949 Hideaki Komiyama [TGB design.]
0950 POSITRON
0951 Koji Takeuchi Graphic Design
0952 PING PONG DESIGN
0953 Zucker & Pfeffer
0954 Fujita Jiro Design
0955 papier colle
0956 Maniackers Design
0957 Koji Takeuchi Graphic Design
0958 Koji Takeuchi Graphic Design
0959 Shintaro Sakamoto
0960 Koji Takeuchi Graphic Design
0961 Megumu Kasuga [YiELD]
0962 Yoshiyuki Sano [HABIT DESIGN]
0963 LOOT
0964 UENO★AMORE★HIROSUKE
0965 Maniackers Design
0966 Yoshiyuki Sano [HABIT DESIGN]
0967 Glashaus Design
0968 MasakuniAraki [papier colle]
0969 papier colle
0970 Tsuyoshi Kusano
©2005 BONES / Project EUREKA・MBS
0971 papier colle
0972 papier colle
0973 SEMITRANSPARENT DESIGN
0974 TOOFLY [Maria Castillo]
0975 Koji Takeuchi Graphic Design
0976 UENO★AMORE★HIROSUKE
0977 Hintzegruppen
0978 PenguinCube
0979 Koji Takeuchi Graphic Design
0980 Tsuyoshi Kusano
0981 Tsuyoshi Hirooka
0982 Tsuyoshi Kusano
0983 Coa Graphics
0984 UENO★AMORE★HIROSUKE
0985 Koji Takeuchi Graphic Design
0986 Patrick Hespeler
0987 Tsuyoshi Kusano
0988 Munehiro Machida [NSSGRAPHICA]
0989 EXTRACT

0990 Shintaro Sakamoto
0991 UENO★AMORE★HIROSUKE
0992 PROTOTYPE DESIGNS
0993 Coa Graphics
0994 Coa Graphics
0995 sylvie lagarde+christophe lavergne [restez vivants!]
0996 papier colle
0997 coma [nadareshiki]
0998 Tsuyoshi Kusano
0999 papier colle
1000 papier colle
1001 papier colle
1002 POSITRON
1003 POSITRON
1004 POSITRON
1005 Tsuyoshi Hirooka
1006 Tsuyoshi Kusano
1007 Jun Watanabe
1008 Tsuyoshi Kusano
1009 Tsuyoshi Hirooka
1010 weissraum.de(sign)
1011 papier colle
1012 Tsuyoshi Hirooka
1013 Tsuyoshi Hirooka
1014 Tsuyoshi Hirooka
1015 POSITRON
1016 Tsuyoshi Hirooka
1017 weissraum.de(sign)
1018 viagrafik
1019 Tsuyoshi Hirooka
1020 Tsuyoshi Hirooka
1021 Hideaki Komiyama [TGB design.]
1022 Ai Fukasawa
1023 POSITRON
1024 WUFFDESIGN
1025 Jakob Holmsberg
1026 STRUKT
1027 POSITRON
1028 Bradley Askew [Smile Maker] / Julia Childs [Pro Wolf Master]
1029 papier colle
1030 PROTOTYPE DESIGNS
1031 Hideaki Komiyama [TGB design.]
1032 Tsuyoshi Hirooka
1033 Ai Fukasawa
1034 Tsuyoshi Hirooka
1035 LOOT
1036 Coa Graphics
1037 123KLAN
1038 inTEAM Graphics
1039 POSITRON
1040 POSITRON
1041 SAFAUSTINA
1042 POSITRON
1043 papier colle
1044 LOOT
1045 A3
1046 Tsuyoshi Kusano
1047 papier colle
1048 LOOT
1049 weissraum.de(sign)
1050 Dainippon Type Organaization

1051 LOOT
1052 Fluid
1053 Kakiko Momokuri
1054 123KLAN
1055 Dopepope
1056 Diverse Designer
1057 substrat
1058 United States of the Art
1059 Dotzero Design
1060 papier colle
1061 Jun Awano [Kaiteki]
1062 papier colle
1063 papier colle
1064 papier colle
1065 papier colle
1066 papier colle
1067 UK_DOUBT [Kentaro Ueno]
1068 papier colle
1069 weissraum.de(sign)
1070 papier colle
1071 papier colle
1072 mikroworld/kibook
1073 Musashi Moriya [The MDP]
1074 POSITRON
1075 Shintaro Sakamoto
1076 Nobuo Yamada
1077 Nobuo Yamada
1078 Gianni Rossi
1079 Gianni Rossi
1080 KIRIE [noriko kirikawa]
1081 Coa Graphics
1082 Nobuo Yamada
1083 UK_DOUBT [Kentaro Ueno]
1084 LOOT
1085 Nobuo Yamada
1086 sylvie lagarde+christophe lavergne [restez vivants!]
1087 Hideaki Komiyama [TGB design.]
1088 Koji Takeuchi Graphic Design
1089 POSITRON
1090 LOOT
1091 EXTRACT
1092 Blutsgeschwister
1093 Hideaki Komiyama [TGB design.]
1094 sylvie lagarde+christophe lavergne [restez vivants!]
1095 3deluxe
1096 EXTRACT
1097 UK_DOUBT [Kentaro Ueno]
1098 Ai Fukasawa
1099 123KLAN
1100 Colin Metcalf and Kevin Grady [GUM]
1101 SUPERDEUX
1102 SUPERDEUX
1103 LOOT
1104 LOOT
1105 LOOT
1106 EXTRACT
1107 Hideaki Komiyama [TGB design.]
1108 123KLAN
1109 POSITRON
1110 Tsuyoshi Kusano
1111 WUFFDESIGN

1112 POSITRON
1113 POSITRON
1114 Diverse Designer
1115 Hideaki Komiyama [TGB design.]
1116 Hitoshi Nagasawa [papier colle]
1117 KENZO MINAMI
1118 KENZO MINAMI
1119 DOPPEL
1120 KENZO MINAMI
1121 SUIKO
1122 SUIKO
1123 LOOT
1124 SUIKO
1125 SUIKO
1126 SUIKO
1127 KENZO MINAMI
1128 123KLAN
1129 DOPPEL
1130 KENZO MINAMI
1131 Yosuke Hamada
1132 LOOT
1133 DOPPEL
1134 ACT
1135 Hitoshi Nagasawa+Yosuke Hamada [papier colle]
1136 Yosuke Hamada
1137 KENZO MINAMI
1138 DOPPEL
1139 KENZO MINAMI
1140 LOOT
1141 DOPPEL
1142 KENZO MINAMI
1143 G [HIROMI SHIGA]
1144 YUKI KOI
1145 YUKI KOI
1146 Symbolon
1147 Symbolon
1148 NICO
1149 Symbolon
1150 Yunico Uchiyama [vesicapisis]
1151 Symbolon
1152 Nobuo Yamada
1153 Symbolon
1154 Nobuo Yamada
1155 Nobuo Yamada
1156 NICO
1157 NICO
1158 ree*rosee
1159 ree*rosee
1160 Yunico Uchiyama [vesicapisis]
1161 Yunico Uchiyama [vesicapisis]
1162 haruna takada
1163 NICO
1164 ROSY-style [Yoshiko Kakuma]
1165 KIRIE [noriko kirikawa]
1166 NICO
1167 KIRIE [noriko kirikawa]
1168 NICO
1169 inTEAM Graphics
1170 Nyarigne
1171 POSITRON
1172 G [HIROMI SHIGA]
1173 UK_DOUBT [Kentaro Ueno]

1174 Nyarigne
1175 Nyarigne
1176 POSITRON
1177 Hitoshi Nagasawa+Eriko Takahashi [papier colle]
1178 Eriko Takahashi
1179 inTEAM Graphics
1180 G [HIROMI SHIGA]
1181 LOOT
1182 123KLAN
1183 Taichi Ito [TARNICA]
1184 weissraum.de(sign)
1185 Taichi Ito [TARNICA]
1186 nem [Shinji Nemoto]
1187 Jun Watanabe
1188 Jun Watanabe
1189 LOOT
1190 POSITRON
1191 LOOT
1192 LOOT
1193 LOOT
1194 Var
1195 Gianni Rossi
1196 Gianni Rossi
1197 Gianni Rossi
1198 milmake
1199 Kakiko Momokuri
1200 LOOT
1201 Kakiko Momokuri
1202 Kakiko Momokuri
1203 Kakiko Momokuri
1204 Keita Soejima
1205 ALLRAID GRAPHICS
1206 LOOT
1207 LOOT
1208 Kakiko Momokuri
1209 PRESENT Design
1210 Jun Watanabe
1211 Dotzero Design
1212 Jun Watanabe
1213 LOOT
1214 Jun Watanabe
1215 Y.S.Planning
1216 Jun Watanabe
1217 milmake
1218 Wataru Osakabe [Lovedesign co.]
1219 Yoshihide Arai [illlllli]
1220 Wataru Osakabe [Lovedesign co.]
1221 Wataru Osakabe [Lovedesign co.]
1222 Wataru Osakabe [Lovedesign co.]
1223 Wataru Osakabe [Lovedesign co.]
1224 Wataru Osakabe [Lovedesign co.]
1225 Wataru Osakabe [Lovedesign co.]
1226 Yoshihide Arai [illlllli]
1227 Wataru Osakabe [Lovedesign co.]
1228 Wataru Osakabe [Lovedesign co.]
1229 Wataru Osakabe [Lovedesign co.]
1230 Yoshihisa Nakai
1231 Anonymous
1232 Yoshihisa Nakai
1233 Yoshihide Arai [illlllli]
1234 Hitoshi Nagasawa [papier colle]

designer index

A

A NEW PERSPECTIVE
yf@anpw.cc
www.anpw.cc

A3
www.athreedesign.com

ACT
actonez6117@yahoo.co.jp

Ai Fukasawa
ai@freshaugust.com
www.freshaugust.com

ALLRAID GRAPHICS
iwata_ar@nifty.com

Amigos
www.amigos.se

ASYL CRACK
crack@asyl.co.jp
www.asyl.co.jp

ASYL DESIGN
contact@asyl.co.jp
www.asyl.co.jp

Aya Naito
a-naito@stf.kodansha.co.jp

Ayako Tsuboi
[Sakurambo Kikaku]
sakurambo@za.pial.jp

B

Bencium Cross Media
www.benicium.hu

Blutsgeschwister
www.blutsgeschwister.de

BooLab.
info@boolab.info
www.boolab.info/

Brandoctor
www.brandoctors.com

C

C100 Studio
www.c100studio.com

C375
www.c375.com

Coa Graphics
coa@coagraphics.com
www.coagraphics.com

Colin Metcalf and Kevin Grady/
[GUM]
editors@gumworld.com
Info@lemonland.net
www.gumworld.com
www.lemonland.net

coma
coma@nadareshiki.com
www.nadareshiki.com

D

Dainippon Type Organaization/
dainippon@type.org
dainippon.type.org

deep llp
www.deep.co.uk

Designgruppe Koop
www.designgruppe-koop.de

Diverse Designer
Dopepope
www.dopepope.com

DOPPEL
info@doppel.to
www.doppel.to

Dotzero Design
www.dotzerodesign.com

E

Emmi Salonen
www.emmi.co.uk

endoko
endoko@thn.ne.jp
www2.tokai.or.jp/funfun

enter98
www.enter98.hu

Eriko Takahashi
comepretty@snet.tvc.jp

Eriko Takahashi+Hitoshi Nagasawa
[papier colle]
papiercolle@nifty.com
www.papiercolle.net

Eskim Dmitry

EXTRACT
www.extract.jp/
info@extract.jp

F

Fluid
www.fluid.nl und Jijzijn
www.jijZijn.nl

Formlos
www.formlos.net

Frank Rocholl
www.rocholl.cc

Fujita Jiro Design
fjd@fides.dti.ne.jp
www.fjd.jp

G

G [HIROMI SHIGA]
sh12027@yahoo.co.jp

Gianni Rossi
www.giannirossi.net

Glashaus Design
www.glashaus-design.com

H

haruna takada
madamhrn2@yahoo.co.jp
dp08112719.lolipop.jp/2/2page.html

Hatsumi Nonaka
free@hyper.ocn.ne.jp

Heath Kane Design
www.heath-kane.com

Hespeler Patrick
www.patrickhespeler.de

Hideaki Kato
imageplot@hotmail.com
www.imageplot.net

Hideaki Komiyama
[TGB design.]
komiyama@tgbdesign.com
www.tgbdesign.com/komiyama

Hintzegruppen
www.hk-gk.dk

Hitoshi Nagasawa
[papier colle]
papiercolle@nifty.com
www.papiercolle.net

I

inTEAM Graphics

J

Jakob Holmsberg
contact@jakobholmsberg.com
jakobholmsberg.com

Jiro Takagi [Haus Graphic]
j.takagi@dream.com

Jun Awano [Kaiteki]
jun@kitk.org
www.kitk.org
www.cryogenicx.com

Jun Watanabe
info@harpoon.jp
www.junwatanabe.jp

K

Kakiko Momokuri
primefleur_ki_ko041984@yahoo.co.jp

Keita Soejima
soeji@kt.rim.or.jp
www.kt.rim.or.jp/~soeji

KENZO MINAMI
agent@cwc-i.com
contact@kenzominami.com
www.kenzominami.com
www.cwc-i.com

KIRIE [noriko kirikawa]
manon@mbg.nifty.com

Koji Takeuchi Graphic Design
info@ktgd.net
ktgd.net

L

Lindedesign
www.lindedesign.de

LOOT
loot@iris.ocn.ne.jp
www5.ocn.ne.jp/~loot

Lowork
info@lowork.com
www.lowork.com

M

Maniackers Design
sato@mks.jp.org
http://mks.jp.org

Marc Atlan Design, Inc.
http://www.marcatlan.com

Masakuni Araki
[papier colle]
papiercolle@nifty.com
www.papiercolle.net

Masashi Ichifuru
[TGB design.]
ichifuru@tgbdesign.com
www.tgbdesign.com/ichifuru

Masato Yamaguchi
[idea sketch international]
yamaguchi@ideasketch.jp
www.works-m-yamaguchi.com

Megumu Kasuga[YiELD]
yield_cad@yahoo.co.jp

Melle/Dorland
www.dorland.de

Mende Design
www.mendedesign.com

mikroworld/kibook
www.mikroworld.com
www.kibook.com

Milkxhake
mix@milkxhake.org
www.milkxhake.org

milmake
design@milmakedesigners.com
www.milmakedesigners.com

Munehiro Machida/
[NSSGRAPHICA]
info@nssgraphica.com
www.nssgraphica.com

Musashi Moriya
[The MDP]
musashi@mdpcrw.com
www.mdpcrw.com

N

nem
s@nneemm.com
www.nneemm.com

NICO
starfactory@dream-more.com
www.nicopop.net

Nobuo Yamada
nobb@xb3.so-net.ne.jp
www006.upp.so-net.ne.jp/abh/

NOK Design
www.nokdesign.com

Nyarigne
avrillavignenyarin@yahoo.co.jp

O

123KLAN
scien-klor@123klan.com
www.123klan.com

12ender GmbH
www.12ender.de

P

papier colle
papiercolle@nifty.com
www.papiercolle.net

Patrick Hespeler

PenguinCube
www.penguincube.com

PING PONG DESIGN
www.pingpongdesign.com

Planet Pixel Cologne
www.planetpixel.de

POSITRON
info@the-positron.com
www.the-positron.com

POWER GRAPHIXX
support@power-graphixx.com
www.power-graphixx.com

PRESENT Design

Pro Wolf Master
Mr.Invisible
Rick Falcon
Julia Childs
info@prowolfmaster.com
http://www.prowolfmaster.com
Bradley Askew [Smile Maker]
http://www.baskrew.com

PROTOTYPE DESIGNS
info@prototypedesigns.org
www.prototypedesigns.org

R

RA GRADI

Red Herring Design
www.redherring.com

red hot'n'cool
www.redhotncool.com

ree*rosee
ree-k@hkg.odn.ne.jp
ameblo.jp/reerosee

Rinzen
www.rinzen.com

Rogerio Lionzo
www.lionzo.com

Rosendahl Grafikdesign
www.rosendahlgrafik.de
ROSY-style
info@rosy-style.com
www.rosy-style.com

S

SAFAUSTINA
www.sfaustina.com

SEMITRANSPARENT DESIGN
info@semitra.com
www.semitransparentdesign.com

Seres Tamas
www.artistamuvek.hu

Shinji Shimada + Akiko Tauchi
[vwv//design]
info@vwv11.com
www.vwv11.com

Shintaro Sakamoto
www.yurayurateikoku.com

SOUP DESIGN
soupdesign@violin.ocn.ne.jp

stilradar
www.stilradar.de

STRUKT
www.strukt.at

substrat
www.substratdesign.org

SUIKO
suiko1@hotmail.com
www.suiko1.com

SUPERDEUX
agent@cwc-i.com
www.superdeux.com
www.cwc-i.com

sylvie lagarde+christophe lavergne
[restez vivants!]
welcome@restezvivants.com
www.restezvivants.com

Symbolon
info@symbolon.jp
www.symbolon.jp

T

Taichi Ito [TARNICA]
info@tarnica.jp
www.tarnica.jp

Takehiko Tsutsumi [ebc]
ttmbox@ebcenter.jp
www.ebcenter.jp

Takeshi Hamada
www.hamada-takeshi.com

ten_do_ten
ten@tententen.net
www.tententen.net

3deluxe
www.3deluxe.de
info@3deluxe.de

TNOP_bePOSI+IVE design

TOOFLY [Maria Castillo]
Toofly@mac.com
www.tooflydesign.com

Tsuyoshi Hirooka
hirooka_tsuyoshi@ybb.ne.jp
hiro-ka.jpn.org

Tsuyoshi Kusano
tsuyos-k@momo.so-net.ne.jp

U

UENO★AMORE★HIROSUKE
amore@love.email.ne.jp
WWW.MONSTER-MIX.COM

UK_DOUBT
UK_DOUBT@yahoo.co.jp

UMBRUCH Gestaltung
www.umbruch.tv

United States of the Art
www.unitedstatesoftheart.com

Urs Lehni
www.our-magazine.ch

V

Var
www.woo.se

viagrafik
www.viagrafik.com

VIER5
www.vier5.de

W

Wataru Osakabe
[Lovedesign co.]
mail@lovedesign.tv

weissraum.de(sign)
www.weissraum.de

White Noise
www.whitenoise.net

WUFFDESIGN
www.wuffdesign.de

Y

Y.S.Planning
ysp@aurora.dti.ne.jp
www.aurora.dti.ne.jp/~ysp/

yo-suke yamamoto
mt_book_sun_go_between@msn.com

Yoshihide Arai [illllli]
info@illllli.com
www.illllli.com
portfolio.illllli.com

Yoshihisa Nakai
kohato@kohato.que.jp
kohato.que.jp

Yoshiyuki Sano
[HABIT DESIGN]
sano@habit-d.com
www.habit-d.com
www.hed.jp

Yosuke Hamada
hamata0712@yahoo.co.jp

Yosuke Hamada
+Hitoshi Nagasawa
papiercolle@nifty.com
www.papiercolle.net

YUKI KOI
info@yukikoi.com
www.yukikoi.com

Yunico Uchiyama
[vesicapisis]
cotton25@r6.dion.ne.jp
yunicof.hp.infoseek.co.jp

Yutaka Tateyama
xjdth44i@yahoo.co.jp

Z

ZERO Headline Advertising
www.zonazero.ru

ZETUEI FONTS
mail@zetuei.com
www.zetuei.com

Zion Graphics
www.ziongraphics.com

Zucker & Pfeffer
www.zuckerundpfeffer.com

Author Profile

Hitoshi Nagasawa

Hitoshi Nagasawa founded a design firm, papier collè with several friends in 1981. Nagasawa is known for designing posters, catalogs, and other paraphernalia for art shows and exhibitions, including the Bauhaus Exhibition. He is also known for leading the planning of the Casio Data Bank product series and designing and producing the typography and icons used with the collection, of which the Casio Wave Ceptor became a huge hit. He is responsible for designing the official website of the National Museum of Art, Osaka (NMAO) and has been involved in a wide range of work, including designing fashion magazines and book covers. His work has been published in the United States by Rockport Publishers in the book *New Design: Tokyo: The Edge of Graphic Design*. The works credited to papier collè appearing in this volume are the collaborative efforts of Hitoshi Nagasawa and Kazutoshi Sakamoto or Hitoshi Nagasawa and Masakuni Araki.

bibliography

1986 *Deviant city, Berlin : From Classical Weimar to Nazism frenzy* (Tairiku Publishing)
1991 *Club and Saloon* (NTT Publishing)
1993 *Dance Beyond The Dance* (JICC)
1998 *The Future of The Body* (TREVILLE)
2000 *past futurama 20th Century, the modern age; its desire and style* (Film Art)
2006 *BIBA Swingin' London 1965-1974* (blues interactions, inc)
2007 *Scratch on the Wall* (blues interactions, inc)

URL. □ http://www.papiercolle.net E-MAIL. □ papiercolle@nifty.com